I0793646

POLLY JESSUP

POLLY JESSUP

Grande Dame of Palm Beach Decorators

Maggie Lidz

Preservation Foundation of Palm Beach
in association with D Giles Limited

WOMEN IN DESIGN
Each book in this series celebrates the untold stories of a woman designer in Palm Beach. The series will feature a range of interior designers, landscape architects, architects, and artists.

© 2025 Preservation Foundation of Palm Beach
© 2025 Maggie Lidz

All rights reserved. No part of the contents of this book may be reproduced, stored in a retrieval system, or transmitted in any form or by any means, electronic, mechanical, photocopying, recording, or otherwise, without the written permission of the Preservation Foundation of Palm Beach and D Giles Limited.

First published in 2025 by
Preservation Foundation of Palm Beach
311 Peruvian Avenue
Palm Beach, Florida 33480
www.palmbeachpreservation.org

Katie Jacob, Vice President

In association with GILES
An imprint of D Giles Limited
66 High Street
Lewes, BN7 1XG, UK
gilesltd.com

Copyedited and proofread by Sarah Kane
Designed by Alfonso Iacurci
Produced by GILES
Printed and bound in China

ISBN: 978-1-913875-95-4

Front cover: Detail of fig. 51
Back cover: Fig. 54
Frontispiece: Detail of fig. 4
Page 4: Detail of fig. 45
Page 7: Polly Jessup pictured on vacation in Europe with her husband, John Jessup. Image from her travel scrapbook donated to PFPB from the Daniels family.

Distributed in the USA and Canada by
Consortium Book Sales & Distribution
The Keg House
34 Thirteenth Avenue, NE, Suite 101
Minneapolis, MN 55413-1007
USA
www.cbsd.com

CONTENTS

6

Acknowledgments

9

Polly Jessup: Grande Dame of Palm Beach Decorators

44

Notable Clients and their Jessup Inc. Rooms

67

Jessup Inc. Employees

73

Selected Bibliography

76

Client List

78

About the Author

79

Index

ACKNOWLEDGMENTS

I am grateful to Polly Jessup's nephew, Ron Daniel, and her grand-nephews, Stephen and David, for initiating this project and providing the funding for its success.

Many thanks to the former staff of Jessup Inc. for so generously sharing their memories: Skip Bermudes, Anne Pepper, Lois Wideman, Mimi McMakin, Hank Brooks, Henry ("Hank") Cochran, and Elizabeth Stewart. Anne Pepper connected me with one of Polly's last clients, Helen Gray. Pepper also guided me to Henry Cochran, who made an extraordinary effort to help, sharing memories and photographs. Draper Paul Maybaum, contracted by Jessup Inc. towards the end of the firm's existence, was patient enough to spend untold hours on the phone with me and made the excellent suggestion to look at Dominick Dunne's *People Like Us*. My special thanks to decorative painter Sharon Gray, daughter of Jack Coon, without whom this book would never have been conceived. Not only was she terribly patient with me and all my questions, but she had the foresight to donate her father's Jessup Inc. furniture inventory to the Preservation Foundation of Palm Beach.

I would not have been able to track down the information in this book without the generous help of Director of Archives Marie Penny and Vice President Katie Jacob at the Preservation Foundation of Palm Beach and Librarian Betse Gori at the Society of the Four Arts. They both were unstinting in sharing their Jessup Collections with me. Many thanks to Director of Research at the Palm Beach Historical Society, Rose Guerrero, for making Polly Jessup's 1987 oral history available.

Lisa Worley and Mark Heppner at the Edsel and Eleanor Ford Museum were invaluable from the beginning of this project, as were Ben Colman, James Hanks, and Maria Ketchum of the Detroit Institute of Arts. Thank you.

The textile historian Deborah Kraak made valuable suggestions including reaching out to Dilys Blum at the Philadelphia Museum of Art. The historian and antiques dealer Amy Finkel helped me contact costume and textile historian Edward Maeder, who greatly assisted me. Through his help I was able to reach curator Anna Jolly at the Abegg-Stiftung, costume curator Sonnet Stanfill at the Victoria and Albert Museum, and coaching historian and former Palm Beach resident Merri Ferrell.

Many thanks to archivist Jason Speck at Hillwood Museum, archivist Melissa Bowling at the Metropolitan Museum of Art, architectural historian Willie Granston, Natalie Shores at Ladew Gardens, Carley C. Altenburger at Winterthur Museum, Thomas Savage at Colonial Williamsburg, and historian and interior designer Gail Winkler.

My appreciation to Louis Bofferding, Barry Cenower, Layla Collins, Jane Day, Emily Eerdmans, Joshua Eldred, Maureen Footer, Leta Austin Foster, Willie Granston, Mac Griswold, Augustus Mayhew, Celia McGee, Isolde Motley, Laura Munder, Mitch Owens, Stephen Salny, Scott Sloat, Jeanne Sloane, Scott Snyder, Martha Stewart, and Susan Vari. Social and architectural historian Jeff Groff helped from the beginning to the end for which I will be always grateful.

Many thanks also to the wise guidance of interior designer Thomas Jayne. At the very beginning of this project, he suggested I contact Skip Bermudes, without whose help I would not have been able to complete this book. As I completed the manuscript, Thomas Jayne's insights have been crucial and I appreciate them very much.

This book is dedicated to Skip Bermudes, Sharon Gray, and my extraordinarily patient husband, Franz Lidz.

Fig. 50 detail. Polly Jessup's living room at 209 Phipps Plaza, Palm Beach.

POLLY JESSUP

Grande Dame of Palm Beach Decorators

Maggie Lidz

Her extravagant insistence upon quality, and quality only, has not been equaled.
—Billy Baldwin, *An Autobiography*, 1985

Introduction

Although her client list included Fords, Whitneys, du Ponts, Kennedys, Mellons, and Pulitzers, the interior designer Polly Jessup has been practically erased from history—partly through her own doing. Born in 1899, Jessup came of age at a time when ladies never courted attention for personal gain. Like the lofty English decorating firm of Colefax and Fowler, she shunned advertising, refused to label her custom work, and declined credit in magazine articles. From the late 1920s to the late 1980s, this business strategy attracted publicity-shy blue chippers who trusted her. "We only do work for people we really care about," said Jessup, a policy that ensured her clients felt part of an exclusive, tasteful community.

She radiated calm in a field where stress and anxiety tend to run high. A tall, composed woman, she was always well groomed: buffed nails, wavy hair "just so," a judicious amount of makeup (lipstick and powder), and understated jewelry (pearls, a brooch, a wedding band). Business associates often described Jessup as motherly, which may account for the tender protectiveness so many employees and clients felt for her. Her former design associate, the now-legendary Billy Baldwin, expressed almost filial concern that his onetime boss was unappreciated. "To list the decorators of America without mentioning Polly Jessup is only murder," he wrote, "because she is one of the very best that we have ever had."

Her elegantly tailored upholstery (Baldwin said they were "the most beautiful curtains of anybody in America or Europe") and peerless reproductions were fashioned in her own Florida workshops. Historian Adam Lewis described Jessup's Palm Beach operation as a "decorating empire." Out-of-town designers such as Ruby Ross Wood, French & Company, Carlhian of Paris, and McMillen relied on Jessup Inc. to oversee their local projects. Jessup's six-decade career was practically a hymn to perseverance: she maintained her standards of quality through the economic downturns of the Great Depression, the building contraction during World War II, and the economic revival of postwar America.

Shortly before her death in 1988, a *New York Times* profile by Anne-Marie Schiro exposed her to a wider audience. "Jessup-ed" was the term used to describe the deceptive simplicity of her rooms. Although the article was entirely laudatory, Jessup shuddered at the recollection during an interview a few weeks later with the Historical Society of Palm Beach County: "We never had publicity until that woman wrote that story."

One domino followed another: Jessup not only spoke to the *Times* and the Historical Society but, after six years of stonewalling, she consented to speak with the director of the new Edsel & Eleanor Ford House, who wanted to chat about her long-time clients, the museum's founders. The rush of interviews at the end of her life suggests that perpetual obscurity may not have been her desire. By the 1980s, her restrained Anglo-French style seemed passé next to the reigning English country house look with its ruffled patterned slipcovers and beribboned portraits of Cavalier King Charles Spaniels. Perhaps Jessup feared what Baldwin had warned about: the tight-lipped circumspection that attracted high-profile clients during her lifetime would undercut her posthumous reputation.

Jessup died on July 24, 1988. She willed the company to her longtime employees, John Hulse and Neal McGinnis. Among the most significant commissions after Polly's death was for Eleanor Ford's granddaughter, Eleanor "Nonie" Ford, and her husband, Frederic Bourke. Hulse and his assistant, Skip Bermudes, worked with the architect Robert A. M. Stern in Aspen. Said to have been among Stern's favorite houses, and the only one in Colorado, the ski lodge was published in the June 1992 issue of *Architectural Digest*. Breaking usual practice, Jessup Inc. was given credit alongside Stern. Despite that success, the company floundered. Hulse and McGinnis did not have the energy to change the business model of Jessup, Inc. which had too many people on the payroll and did not take deposits.

After five years Hulse and McGinnis retired and cleared out the buildings. The extensive business archives—six decades of client books, commission ledgers, and personnel records—were destroyed. "John and Neal tore them up little by little," said Skip Bermudes, then an assistant designer to Hulse. "They had no choice."

Using what remains, this book attempts to position Jessup in the pantheon of twentieth-century designers. I draw on the collection of drawings and photos at the Preservation Foundation of Palm Beach, the photos at the Society of the Four Arts, the oral history at the Historical Society of Palm Beach County, a miscellany of documents in Michigan, and finally, the memories shared by her family, employees, friends, clients, and business associates. They paint a picture of an indomitable woman, a model of kindness. These witnesses were unanimous in praising her generosity and stubborn integrity. One anecdote from interior designer Mimi McMakin sums it up neatly:

> 'Late in life, while driving in West Palm Beach, Jessup took a wrong turn and found herself on an on-ramp to a busy highway. Uncharacteristically startled, she brought her car to a dead stop, causing a backup. A state trooper pulled over and strode to the driver's side window. "Lady," he said, "the sign says to yield, not surrender."'

Jessup, of course, was incapable of surrender (fig. 1).

Before Jessup Inc.

Jessup's career as an interior designer to the privileged had an unlikely trajectory. She was the first of three children born in Hartford, Connecticut, to Katharine Galloway, daughter of an Irish-Protestant barkeep from Philadelphia, and David Daniel, a Jewish clothing merchant who grew up in Mississippi. The marriage would have been considered "mixed" by the standards of the time, as Jewish people were considered as much of a race—with distinct physical, intellectual, and moral characteristics—as a religion. Perhaps to reassure customers, Daniel announced in a *Hartford Courant* advertisement on December 25, 1908 that his employees had been given the day off, and the Daniel home had a large Christmas tree. Such nods to Christianity would not have insulated his family from antisemitism, which the ad appears to have attempted to deflect. Switching religion wasn't an option. For example, the conversion to Catholicism of Daniel's New England contemporary, Bernard Berenson (1865-1959), did not alter the status of the Harvard-trained art historian as a Jewish person, even to himself. Berenson wrote about Henry Adams, the author and Boston Brahmin, "We had much in common, but he could not forget that he was an Adams and was always more embarrassed than I was that I happened to be a Jew."

Throughout most of the twentieth century, "success" required following rules established by Adams and his peers, the so-called WASP (White Anglo-Saxon Protestant) Ascendency. Its exclusive schools and clubs—which barred Jews, Catholics, Blacks, Asians, Hispanics, the Irish, southern Europeans and women—were where information was exchanged, contacts made, and business transacted. The racist quotas of the 1924 Johnson Act effectively cut off immigration from South and Eastern Europe in the hope of keeping America a Protestant nation. WASP men controlled the executive suites of businesses, universities, government, and museums. The way they, their wives, and their children lived and behaved was more than just grist for the national gossip mill. The details could be deployed for social mobility and financial self-improvement. This accounts for why golf became a favored game for businessmen, why immigrants in all forty-eight states filled their houses with Colonial Revival furniture, and why ethnic names were "Americanized."

The Daniel children employed various strategies to keep antisemitism at bay. The youngest child and only male, David Richard Daniel (1902-1967), simply ignored his Jewish roots. When he was eight days old,

Fig. 1
Pauline "Polly" Jessup (1899–1988) in her Palm Beach home office. Details were everything at Jessup, Inc. The floors were antique Cuban tile and the wall paneling glazed with wax crayons. Each set of curtains was hung with a scalloped and fringed valance, and then punctuated with a disc-shaped curtain pin. A swag and tail appearance was created with the terra-cotta–colored cords, which were finished with tasseled bobbins. Courtesy of the Daniel Family, Preservation Foundation of Palm Beach (PFPB).

his parents formally welcomed him into the Jewish community, a festivity that may have been intended to please his elderly paternal grandparents. After this occasion, religious trappings of Judaism seem to have been dropped. Young David worshiped in the Episcopalian church of his mother, married a gentile, and eventually became publisher of the city's afternoon daily, *The Hartford Times*. His oldest sister, Pauline ("Polly") Daniel, also married a gentile. In 1925, she assumed, as was customary, her husband's impeccably Protestant last name. The middle child, Margaret, took the most active stance to protect herself. She invented an uber-WASP middle name and anglicized the family name by adding an *S* to the end. As Margaret Harrington Daniels, she worked as a researcher at the Metropolitan Museum of Art. She, too, eventually married a gentile.

Antisemitism was so ubiquitous that few at the time objected to, or even noticed, the characterization of Jewish people in such beloved American novels as Edith Wharton's 1905 *House of Mirth* (the Shylock-like banker Simon Rosedale, who speaks ungrammatically and wears clothes that "fit like upholstery") and F. Scott Fitzgerald's 1925 *Great Gatsby*. Fitzgerald modeled Meyer Wolfsheim on the sophisticated, real-life racketeer Arnold Rothstein. In order to make his fictional gangster fit ethnic preconceptions, Fitzgerald made his manners utterly repellant. The slur "kike" was defined by New York–Palm Beach banker and model for the board game figure Mr. Monopoly, Otto Kahn, as "a Jewish gentleman who has just left the room."

Nazism, perversely, deepened American antisemitism. The Oscar-winning 1947 film *Gentleman's Agreement* exposed the subtle and overt anti-Jewish mores of polite society. The movie was considered so daring that the star Gregory Peck (christened Eldred and raised Catholic) was advised by his agent not to accept the role.

Hobe Sound, where Mrs. John Colgate Jessup was embraced as the interior designer of choice, was, in the words of one satisfied gentile, "strictly non-Jew." Jewish people were not invited to join the island's private club, which Jessup had decorated and around which island life revolved. Though Jews could be hosted on the island, they were basically stanchioned to the house in which they were guests, in contrast to WASP visitors, who were cordially welcomed everywhere and given temporary privileges at the club.

Enforcing standards of ethnic purity could be complicated. Marie Whitney, second wife of tycoon and Hobe Sound stalwart Averell Harriman, was advised to keep quiet about her Jewish grandfather. She responded by boycotting the club. Another notoriously restricted place was Palm Beach's Everglades Club, where Polly was a member for more than a half century, but Kahn had never been permitted. Ironically, if her father's religion had been known, Polly would have been blackballed from the venues she decorated and barred from purchasing

Fig. 2
Advertisement for "Dave Daniel's Modern Clothes Shop" in *The Hartford Courant*, December 22, 1911.

houses in neighborhoods where she worked on a regular basis.

Childhood

Until Polly was twelve, her family was flush with cash. The Daniels lived in downtown Hartford with at least one live-in servant and a chauffeur. They were not part of Hartford society, gentile or Jewish. Polly's father, an early member of the Hartford Automobile Club, raced sleighs, horses, and the newfangled motor cars. In 1905, when Polly was six, her parents drove a Model F Cadillac to New York, a newsworthy event. Until 1910, David Daniel and his brother Harry owned a chain of stores, H & D Daniel Clothing. When Polly was twelve, her father and uncle dissolved the partnership. David was forced into bankruptcy. He launched a second business almost immediately, but the family's former prosperity was gone. "I don't know anything but buying and selling clothes," he announced in one of his ads, which offered cotton serge

"I knew fabrics because I was trained in it," Polly said about her early years. Her sister Peggy, who became a textile historian, donated more than two dozen items from her wardrobe to the costume collection in London's Victoria and Albert Museum. The clothes were (and are) prized as superlative examples of twentieth-century women's tailoring.

Fig. 3
The elegant Daniel sisters, dark-haired Polly (left) and blonde Peggy on a European holiday in 1935. Both jump-started their careers by trading in their knowledge of textiles, which they gleaned from their father as children. Courtesy of the Daniel Family, PFPB.

suits, worsted wool jackets, cashmere pants, and silk-lined overcoats (fig. 2).

Upon graduation from Hartford Public High School, the Daniel girls landed jobs at local insurance agencies, a step up from factory work—but just barely. At the turn of the century, almost two-thirds of American working women were domestic servants. In the wake of World War I and the suffragette movement, more middle- and upper-class women attended colleges, but the coeds weren't expected to work. When Sister Parish decided to become a professional interior decorator in 1933, her husband was disinherited by an aunt because his wife "went into trade." The aunt's largesse was instead bestowed on a cousin, Eleanor Roosevelt. Evidently, being a Democrat was less of a disgrace than being a woman who accepted money for labor (fig. 3).

Unlike Parish, the Daniel girls had no rich, WASP relatives to offend. They also didn't intend to stay clerks in Hartford forever. Peggy and Polly moved to New York in 1922. Peggy found work as an assistant in the lantern-slide library at the Met; Polly, at the National Birth Control League. Her boss was Margaret Sanger,

Fig. 4
Polly Daniel Jessup and her wedding ring, 1930s. Courtesy of the Daniel Family, PFPB.

whose cultured persona and ability to speak gracefully about this once-forbidden subject attracted widespread support among doctors, religious leaders, writers, and society figures. ("There is nothing in her lecture to offend," wrote one journalist.) In September 1923, Polly represented Sanger in Chicago. Over the next year, Polly's tact and common sense—traits that would be remarked on the rest of her life—made her a popular speaker at ladies' club events.

Polly and John

Sometime before 1925, practical Polly fell in love with a charming, older married man. Matinee-idol handsome with dark hair and blue eyes, John Colgate Jessup Jr. was twenty-six years her senior. His middle name derived from John Colgate, an early business partner of his grandfather. To the (literal) misfortune of his descendants, the grandfather eventually fell out with the soap-making clan. He opened a paint-manufacturing plant. Colgate-Palmolive is now, of course, one of the world's largest conglomerates. Jessup Paints dried up long ago (figs. 4 and 5).

John attended a prestigious private boarding school, Phillips Academy-Andover. After graduating in 1895, he went to the University of Rochester, where he studied engineering. Four years later he matriculated briefly at Brown University. After leaving college (he never graduated), John wound up in Manhattan and joined The Foundation Company, which specialized in subaquatic building. In 1906, he married Louise Foote, a twenty-nine-year-old Vassar graduate, and they had two children within two years.

The dangerous work of tunneling adversely affected John's health, necessitating a career change. By 1915, John worked as a bond salesman at New York's Guaranty Trust Company.
As John prospered, he moved his family from Brooklyn to Buffalo to Harrisburg, Pennsylvania. In February 1920, he was promoted to head of the Hartford office.

Fig. 5
John Colgate Jessup, 1920s.
Courtesy of the Daniel Family, PFPB.

"Mr. and Mrs. David Daniel of No. 490 Farmington Avenue announce the marriage of their daughter, Miss Pauline Daniel to John C. Jessup of Olympia, Florida on Saturday at West Palm Beach, Florida. Mr. and Mrs. Jessup will live in Olympia."

***Hartford Courant*, Monday, April 27, 1925**

Four years later, he abruptly changed direction. John and Louise separated. He took off for Florida, which John (and many other would-be land speculators) called "the last pioneer state." That summer he teamed up with Morland Horsfall, whose wife, Ruth, was an old friend of Peggy Daniel (a relationship that was almost certainly connected to Polly's future marriage). Morland and John bought and sold real estate in the freshly minted town of Olympia, about thirty-five miles north of Palm Beach.

The brainchild of real estate mogul Malcolm Meacham, the Olympia Improvement Corporation was bankrolled by a group of investors that included the Biddle and Duke families. Anthony Joseph ("Tony") Drexel Biddle Jr. was installed as president, and Swiss architect Maurice Fatio came down from New York to design the new island community. Streets were laid out and named after Greco-Roman gods: Apollo, Venus, Athena, Mars. An ersatz town hall served as the corporate sales office. A dilapidated men's club was remodeled into a fancy winter resort. Although it strains credulity (six years later, Permelia Reed stayed there and described it as "fearfully run down"), a January 1925 advertisement in *Vogue* boasted that the Olympia Beach Inn featured a French restaurant, a nine-hole golf course, and bathrooms and telephones in all eighty rooms.

Fig. 6
Picture City advertisement, *The Miami Daily News*, October 28, 1925.

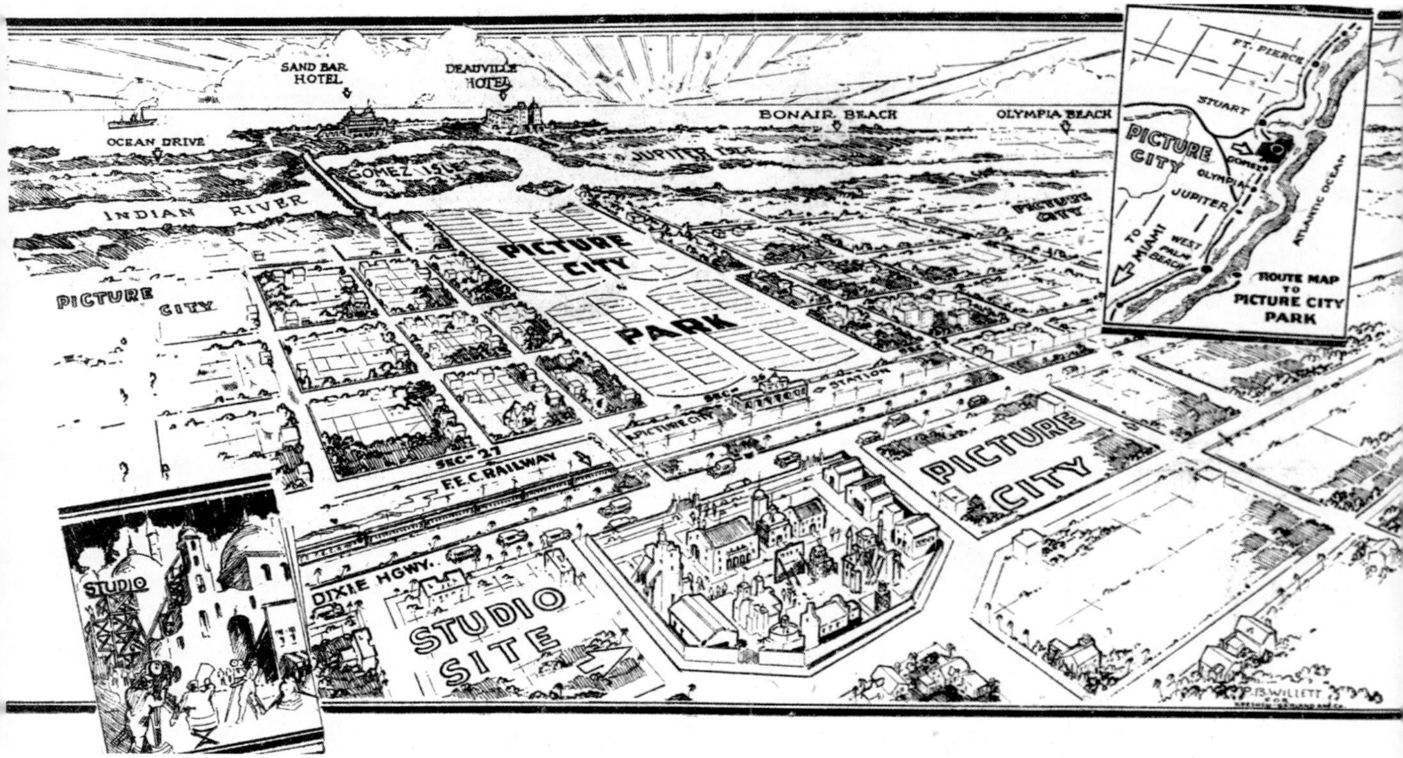

The winter of 1924–25 was the peak of the South Florida land boom. John filed for divorce from Louise that March. He married Polly in April. Sanger's letter of congratulation alluded to Polly's long wait: "It's just fine Polly dear that you two are together at last. John's love is the sort that lasts through the ages, when it's taken care of a little."

The house John planned as their honeymoon cottage was completed just before the wedding. Furnishing it, however, was frustrating. The increased construction in the state caused months-long delivery delays. At one point, all non-emergency cargo was embargoed to reduce the railroad yard logjam. John suggested that he and Polly build their own furniture. "That was really the way it started," Polly recalled in her oral history at the Palm Beach Historical Society. "We got a couple of carpenters, and we built some very simple, out of pecky cypress, tables and benches and four-poster beds and chests . . . very makeshift . . . but attractive." John enjoyed his new hobby, and Polly did too. As a lark, Polly said, she began helping friends with their houses.[1]

The future seemed to hold endless possibilities. In July, the Olympia Improvement Corporation was bought out by a star-dusted syndicate headed by the film producer Lewis J. Selznick and his partner, Joseph Schenck,

Fig. 7
The run on the Farmer's Bank, *The Palm Beach Post*, March 9, 1927.

CROWDS GREET ARMORED CAR

Traffic was temporarily blocked on Clematis street at 11 o'clock yesterday morning when an armored car (indicated by the arrow) under heavy guard, arrived from Miami bearing $1,000,000 in cash reinforcements for the Farmers Bank and Trust company. Throngs of persons gathered around the car, and a pathway had to be forced by the police to allow guards to transfer the money into the bank vaults.

president of United Artists. The Selznick group planned to create a 250-acre movie studio to the west of Olympia that would rival Hollywood. The prospect of UA founders D. W. Griffith, Mary Pickford, Douglas Fairbanks, and Charlie Chaplin sunning themselves in nearby beach cabanas must have excited John, Polly, and their fellow Olympians. The town's name was changed—overly optimistically, it turned out—to Olympia-Picture City (fig. 6).

Hopes for Olympia-Picture City were dashed not long after the sale. The South Florida land boom, always volatile, turned bust. A series of devastating hurricanes in 1926 scuttled the studio scheme. John's real estate career sank with it. The land was suddenly worthless. John and Polly relocated to Palm Beach to ponder their next move.

"Don't talk about those lovely early days!" said Polly about the cascade of disasters that she and

John endured. While they were having breakfast on March 8, 1927, some friends, the opera singers Mildred and George Dunstan, stopped by:

> "John, do you have any money in Farmer's Bank?"
>
> "Yes, I do, George. Why?"
>
> "Well, you'd better get down there as fast as you can. That bank is going to close."
>
> John snapped: "It's people like you, George, who start rumors. Certainly the banks will close if you go around saying that."
>
> John didn't get down there fast. Or slow. Or at all. And by noon, all of his and Polly's savings were gone.
>
> They lost everything.
>
> "Incredible, isn't it? Polly recalled. "Nobody owned anything."

The March 1927 bank closure was the beginning of Polly's and John's serious money woes. In August, a court ordered John to pay his ex-wife, Louise, $4,125 (the equivalent of about $68,000 in today's money). Horsfall had his Cadillac repossessed. The Biddle-Dukes foreclosed on the Hollywood syndicate. Meacham's losses were so great he committed suicide. John reconsidered his future in real estate sales (fig. 7).

Jessup Inc. —The Early Years

Almost immediately after the bank failure, and with little more than the memory of their widely admired Picture City house, Polly and John formed a furniture-making business: Jessup Inc. John was president; Polly, secretary. In the beginning, Jessup Inc. consisted of only two workshops: wood and upholstery. He oversaw the furniture; she, the upholstery. E. Reeves Euler, who later became an artist in Provincetown, Rhode Island, was art director and draftsman. At the end of 1927, Jessup Inc. announced the completion of its first commission for the new Palm Beach National Bank. Fatio, whom the Jessups knew from the Picture City fiasco, was the architect. On opening, John placed a congratulatory advertisement in *The Palm Beach Post*. Euler was credited, but not Polly. Nor was she mentioned in a subsequent *Post* article on the new company (fig. 8).

As secretary and wife of the president, Polly may not have been a salaried employee. In Polly's later years, she regaled her staff with tales of clerking in a posh Palm Beach chocolate shop. According to her, the company started after she was asked by a customer who was closing her house for the season to oversee the installation of some curtains while she was away. Polly was desperate for the work; the chocolate shop would soon shutter for the summer. On her return the next winter, the woman was pleased with the results. Word spread that Polly Jessup knew decorating (fig. 9).

The company was first located in the manufacturing district of West Palm Beach,

Fig. 8
Interior view of the First National Bank, circa 1930. PFPB.

Fig. 9
Jessup Inc. sign. Courtesy of Sharon Gray, PFPB.

not far from the ironworks of Addison Mizner, the architect credited with the Mediterranean Revival look of early Palm Beach. Besides an ironworks and architectural office, Mizner had a tileworks, a cabinetmaking shop, and an upholstery studio, which he incorporated in 1925 as Mizner Industries. Mizner's company declared bankruptcy in 1926, was rescued in 1927, and went bankrupt again after his death in 1933. His artisans left for the relative stability of Jessup Inc. Even Edward C. Peters, Mizner's head stonemason, latched on briefly before returning to the resurrected Mizner Industries in 1934 as the

Fig. 10
Carving samples from an early and undated (1927–1930) Jessup Inc. furniture catalog. The photos in the catalog were by Ray B. Dame, who worked closely with Mizner. The Society of the Four Arts, Gioconda and Joseph King Library Collection.

plant's general manager. A decorative plaster block with Addison Mizner's monogram was found when the Jessup Inc. workshops closed in 1993, perhaps bought at one of the Mizner going-out-of-business sales or left by a worker.

Like a medieval guild, the hierarchy within each shop consisted of a foreman at the top, assistants in the middle and, at the bottom, trainees. Perhaps chastened by Mizner's spectacular undoing, the Jessups kept a watchful eye on their balance sheet. Accountants tracked each transaction, and every employee—from woodcarver to down-stuffer—was required to document the hours spent on each job (figs. 10 and 11).

Jessup Inc.'s furniture, like Mizner's, was manufactured to withstand Florida humidity. Flawless reproductions rather than original creations were Jessup Inc.'s forte: extra chairs for antique dining sets; a sofa to match a preexisting one; a duplicated case piece for a more symmetrical room arrangement. Room paneling, built-in bars, coffered ceilings, and elaborately carved "Spanish" or "Italian" doors were also created. Machines with revolving brooms and brushes artificially aged new products. An

Fig. 11
Door from an early and undated (1927–1930) Jessup Inc. furniture catalog. The Society of the Four Arts, Gioconda and Joseph King Library Collection.

Fig. 12
A Knole-style sofa made and upholstered by Jessup Inc., circa 1930. The price depended on whether the customer wanted it in damask as shown ($750) or in muslin ($460), outer fabric chosen later. Absent from this model were the cords that lowered or raised the sofa arms. Cord color, thickness, and number of tassels would be determined by the purchaser. The Society of the Four Arts, Gioconda and Joseph King Library Collection.

electric, Rube Goldberg–like contraption in a walled-off corner of the upholstery shop blasted pounds of virtually weightless down into muslin bags for seating cushions and mattresses. An undated, circa 1930 catalog shows the products of Jessup Inc. as a Mizner-esque mishmash: carved Spanish chests, Italian X frame stools, French provincial settees, and fringed Renaissance chairs. The earliest pieces were stamped with the company name, a practice that soon ceased (fig. 12).

Architects realized that the Jessups could get things done on time and within budget. In January 1927, Woolworth heiress Jessie Donahue decided she wanted a Palm Beach residence built from scratch that would be ready to move into by Christmas. Architect Marion Sims Wyeth and interior designer Elsie Sloan Farley enlisted pretty much every craftsperson in town to help complete what the Donahues christened Cielito Lindo, or Little Piece of Heaven. (One can only imagine what the laborers called it.) It's unclear where the Jessup Inc. furniture was deployed within the 125 rooms and 45,000 square feet, but the Donahues were named as early clients of the company.

In those days, John was the public face of Jessup Inc. His Andover education helped abet the illusion that the company was less about making money than it was a gentleman's occupation. As at Guaranty Trust, long-term connections were cultivated, and deals were sealed with handshakes. Deposits were not taken, and no bills were sent until the project was complete.

White, articulate, and well dressed, the Jessups looked and sounded like, or sometimes better than, their well-heeled customers. As Tom Wolfe noted in *Bonfire of the Vanities,* to attend to their well-being, "old-line, well-fixed" Protestants preferred their own kind. Polly's Connecticut roots were often brandished in conversation, but her Jewish shopkeeper father (alive and in business until 1931) was not mentioned. In the oral history she gave in 1987, she alluded to a grandfather who was an architect in Philadelphia (not true) and childhood vacations in Europe (unlikely). The embellished tales may have been repeated so often that they acquired a greater reality than her father's discount clothing store. More importantly, the misty whiff of genteel affluence attracted the sort of people she and John wanted as clients.

A Silver Lining

Late in the summer of 1928, the Jessups concluded that their efforts were not paying off. John wanted to leave Florida, perhaps go back to engineering. "I've had enough pioneering," he told Polly. But they had one more job to complete. Fatio had enlisted their help on Casa della Porta, a new winter home for the Hudson Automotive president William J. McAneeny and his wife, Susan Peck. The New York interior decorator Ruth Campbell Bigelow (she would start a tea company during the slow years of the Depression that is still run by her descendants) had Jessup Inc. manufacture the woodwork and furniture (figs. 13 and 14).

All plans changed on September 17, 1928, when a hurricane—one of the deadliest to make landfall in South Florida history—caused massive flooding in Palm Beach. For weeks afterward, fish swam in the streets and rubber waders were the footwear of choice. In the storm's aftermath, local architects received a tsunami of telegrams from their northern clients. A common refrain: "Make repairs regardless of cost." John and his men were desperately needed. And Polly found herself suddenly in demand as insurance companies hired her to assess damage. "I was really one of the very few that knew a piece of damask from a velvet," Polly said. But there was a hitch. Polly and John lacked cash for materials.

Polly headed to New York, alone. "I went there with all these smelly things soaked in water and mildew," she recalled. "I needed a hundred yards of this and two hundred yards of that." She paid a visit to the fabric-and-wallpaper manufacturer Johnson and Faulkner (later known as Jofa and, since 1966, as Lee Jofa). Company founder Edward D. Faulkner had died the previous summer and bequeathed the company to six employees. They wouldn't help until Polly pleaded: "There must have been a time that you got started, too." The new owners relented and extended the necessary credit. Flush with capital, the workshops were moved to the three buildings left standing on Georgia Avenue after the hurricane. The company, which would remain there for the next sixty-five years, was back in business.

Polly said that, in the wake of the hurricane, "Jessup Inc. didn't create rooms, it restored what was there." Polly and John took commissions for the Mizner-designed houses of publisher Barclay Warburton and department store heir Rodman Wanamaker (both of Philadelphia), Wyeth's house for utilities magnate Clarence Geist (also based in Philadelphia), and William Lawrence Bottomley's only identified Palm Beach residence designed for the New York yachtsman Kenneth Van Riper and his wife Beatrice. The experience changed the lives of Polly and John, and not just because of their sudden solvency.

As part of a classical art education, students are often asked to copy the work of past masters. This tradition is viewed as one of the most effective ways to transfer artistic skills, giving

Fig. 13
McAneeny dining room at Casa della Porta. PFPB.

Fig. 14
Dining room set in the Jessup Inc. catalog. The Society of the Four Arts, Gioconda and Joseph King Library Collection.

Fig. 15
In the Jessup Inc. files under "Hard Window Valances" was this photo of a British period room in an unknown museum. Courtesy of Anne Pepper, PFPB.

Fig. 16
Undated Jessup Inc. drawing of a similar carved cornice to the one in the British period room for Joseph and Permelia Reed, Greenwich, Connecticut. Courtesy of Anne Pepper, PFPB.

insight into inspiration and technique. At Jessup Inc., Polly and John copied museum furniture from photographs to sell to customers seduced by time-sanctioned styles. In a similar manner, the post-hurricane room restoration taught the couple about interior design (figs. 15 and 16).

Interior design is less about matching colors than organizing space. It's not about placing items where they will look best, but where they will work best. It might look good to have a cluster of little tables in front of the sofa, but they are ridiculous if you can't make your way through them gracefully to sit down, or, more aptly, the butler can't easily pass a tray of hors d'oeuvres to a guest. "Suitability is the test of good taste always," wrote Emily Post in her 1922 *Etiquette*. The experience of effortlessness is the goal of good interior design. The result should be an absence of problems: a seemingly inevitable furniture arrangement, lamps that cast light exactly where needed, every drawer and door opening smoothly.

Good taste, like good design, tends to be case specific. When the German prince and British admiral Louis of Battenberg visited the White House in 1905, he condescendingly complemented its "quiet good taste." He might have approved less if recent renovations by McKim, Mead & White had competed in gilded splendor with the Grand Ducal Castle in Darmstadt where Battenberg married Queen Victoria's granddaughter. What was suitable for a European palace would have been preposterous for a presidential residence, just as diamonds were proper at night but not in the day; a butler must be clean-shaven, but a chef could sport a mustache; and white was not worn after Labor Day (except in the tropics).

The confusing rules about suitability and good taste made *Etiquette* a standard reference book for everyone from millionaires and their private secretaries to bus drivers and their passengers. In Europe, class was determined almost irrevocably at birth. In the more fluid society of the United States, class was about knowledge and taste, a situation profitably exploited by Post, the publisher Condé Nast, and interior designer Elsie de Wolfe. For the Jessups, the intense labor of 1928 was a year-long tutorial in how the very rich lived—and how they aspired to live.

Quiet: The Only Kind of Taste That Mattered

One of the most influential books on twentieth-century American interior design was actually published in 1897. The stated aim of *The Decoration of Houses*, the book Wharton wrote with architect Ogden Codman Jr., was to eliminate the vulgar. This was a "difficult task" (their words), because "vulgarity is always noisier than good breeding." The book's primary targets were the Vanderbilts. Wharton and Codman were relatively poor compared to that family and the hundreds of other newly minted millionaires crowding the ballrooms of New York, but they compensated with hauteur based on their ancestral wealth.

Being well born was one reason Wharton and Codman felt so confident in their opinions. Codman tracked the lineage of the "First Families of Boston," one of which was, unsurprisingly, his own. The more confident Wharton maintained in her autobiography

> "Taste attaches but two conditions to the use of objects of art: that they shall be in scale with the room, and that the room shall not be overcrowded with them. There are two ways of being in scale: there is the scale of proportion, and what might be called the scale of appropriateness. The former is a matter of actual measurement, while the latter is regulated solely by the nicer standards of taste."
>
> **Edith Wharton and Ogden Codman Jr., *The Decoration of Houses*, 1897**

Fig. 17 An eighteenth-century British melon tureen next to a loop chair in the eclectic drawing room of Jessup Inc. clients John B. and Marylou Ford. The Society of the Four Arts, Gioconda and Joseph King Library Collection.

> **"Taste can be either moral or aesthetic, or in really bad cases, both. When it is ethical, it refers to our behavior or to what we say; when it is artistic, it is aimed at what we own."**
>
> **Quentin Crisp, "Taste Be Damned," *House & Garden*, August 1989**

that good breeding was less a birthright than a learned attitude that meant being "careful of the accepted formulas." Wharton and Codman were unwavering in their joint conviction that the highly publicized silver-plated bathtubs of the Vanderbilts rendered them tasteless vulgarians.

Good taste, the physical manifestation of good breeding, was always hushed. It was twisted into a civic virtue in the 1913 guide *The House in Good Taste*, which Ruby Ross Wood ghostwrote for de Wolfe. Tasteful people may have faults, "but they never will cause a scandal!" Restraint in all things was a requirement of taste. Beige and pastels exemplified taste, but color, like money, was fine if washed by age. The rules of taste were as convoluted and as full of exceptions as English grammar. Orchids sometimes had lurid blooms, but their rarity obliterated the gaudiness (fig. 17).

Sometimes logic didn't apply. Among the most inexplicable totems of refinement were antique porcelain vegetables. Expensive and relatively small, the Marie Antoinette-like bibelots were a twentieth-century rage among women who rarely ventured into the kitchen or scrubbed soil from their fingernails. Elizabeth, the Queen Mother, and her mortal enemy, the Duchess of Windsor, were mad for them. Style icons and Jessup Inc. clients Bernice Chrysler Garbisch, Anne Ford, and Jayne Wrightsman used them as decoration for their dining tables and drawing rooms. Another Jessup Inc. patron, Josephine Ford (Mrs. Walter Buhl), dotted her Grosse Point house with eighteenth-century Dutch Delft grapes, English Longton Hall melons, and German Meissen peaches. Only fellow connoisseurs guessed their value. Despite the efforts of Post, Wood, De Wolfe, and others, good taste was never meant to be inclusive.

In his 1922 satire *Babbitt*, Sinclair Lewis skewered the formulaic boundaries of good taste, which he encapsulated in the living room of his anxiety-ridden antihero: "Though there was nothing in the room that was interesting, there was nothing that was offensive. It was as neat and negative as a block of artificial ice."

Caution—even fear—has always been an element of good taste, which offers protection to those who think they need it. When Jacqueline Kennedy—young, Catholic, and a Democrat—moved into the White House, she hired the crusty WASP interior designer Sister Parish (another ceramic vegetable collector) to redo the family quarters. When Kennedy began to redecorate the public rooms, she asked Henry Francis du Pont—elderly, Protestant, and a

Fig. 18

The dawn-like pinky creams and pale blues of Polly's bedroom, where she mixed European antiques with a just-introduced streamlined Princess phone. A gilded call bell, positioned just behind the phone, alluded to her live-in help. The pleated skirt on the tufted chair and looped and tasseled window valance have a tailored rigidity, reminiscent of the stiff, high-crowned coiffures popular in the early '60s when the room was put together. PFPB.

Republican—to chair her committee. With this socially prominent expert on American period rooms in charge, Kennedy said, "There would be no criticism." As Lewis had observed forty years before, the blunting of disapproval—not beauty—was the goal of good taste. A room in good taste functioned as a backdrop. Du Pont's design mantra: Anything that attracts the eye should be removed. Similarly, another White House design advisor to Kennedy, the porcelain-vegetable-loving Bunny Mellon, said: "Nothing should be seen." To the uninitiated, her statement sounded like a Zen koan, but for those in the know, it made perfect sense, just as ceramic vegetables in the drawing room were in good taste, but live petunias in the garden were not (fig. 18).

Jessup Inc. in the 1930s

To outsiders, the town of Palm Beach looked dead in the summer. Stores and restaurants shuttered; churches reduced their hours. For those in the building trades, summertime was the busiest time of the year. Sea air deteriorated metals, textiles, and paint, and houses needed frequent refurbishment. Much of the furniture at Jessup Inc. was constructed from May to December, some of it stored for the January deluge. The Palm Beach season began after Christmas. Luxury stores opened and provided the winter resort community with one of the swankiest (temporary) shopping streets in the world.

In 1930, Elizabeth Arden and Maison de Blanc (linens) were Jessup Inc.'s neighbors when the company opened its seasonal retail outlet on Via Parigi. New stock furniture was offered as well as a carefully selected assortment of antiques and objets d'art. A strolling millionaire could impulsively snatch up a crystal box for cigarettes, a velvet-covered side chair, or a cloisonné vase. Down the street, he or she could purchase a carved emerald necklace (Black, Starr & Frost), a diamond tiara (Cartier), or platinum cufflinks (Udall & Ballou). Nightly parties and monthly balls provided a place to display such glittering bijoux. During Prohibition, the town's biggest bootlegger masked his enterprise with a shingle that read "Dressmaker."

The dominant image of the 1930s is breadlines, but it was during this decade that Jessup Inc. transformed from furniture manufacturing into interior design and seasonal residential services. In 1929, six full-time cabinetmakers and two carvers made up the Jessup Inc. staff. By 1931, that number had shot up to forty.[2] By 1934, the Jessups were able to purchase all three buildings at 6100 Georgia Avenue: one was the office and upholstery, one was the woodshop, and one was for storage.

Polly started the drapery shop after the hurricane. Fabric expanded and shrunk in the South Florida weather, which created havoc with curtain lengths. Polly had hangers installed at

> **"I keep stressing what the workshops represent."**
>
> **Polly Jessup, Oral History at the Historical Society of Palm Beach County, 1988**

Fig. 19
Crossed draperies and alcove draperies from Pierre de La Mésangère's *Meubles et objets de goût* (Paris, 1802–07) from the Jessup Inc. files. Bookshelves in the Jessup Inc. offices contained a range of historical sources as inspiration and direction: Percy Macquoid and Ralph Edward's *Dictionary of English Furniture* (1924–27), Roger de Felice's 1920s series on French furniture, and Giuseppe Morazzoni's 1955 opus on neoclassical Italian furniture. There were reprints of George Smith's *The Cabinet Maker and Upholsterer's Guide* (London, 1826) and Thomas Hope's *Household Furniture and Interior Decoration* (1807), as well as contemporary writings by Paul Frankl, Nancy McClelland, and John Cornforth. Courtesy of Anne Pepper, PFPB.

Jessup Inc., where full-scale paper models could be hoisted and checked for proportion, length, and design. After the fabric was cut and lined, the curtains were rechecked before hemming. She disliked seeing nuts and bolts in a finished room and usually hid drapery rods, rings, and pulleys behind a decorative valance. This could be a flat, thin wood cornice; a deep, curved upholstery pelmet; or something in between (fig. 19).

Polly and John oversaw each commission from the drafting board to installation and annual upkeep. Jessup Inc.'s distinctive brown truck, with its tan-lettered logo, signified doting care to the firm's increasingly devoted customers. With servants in short supply, Jessup

Inc. shouldered work previously performed by housekeepers. Polly employed Mabel West, who arrived at houses with a crew as soon as the owner departed. They readied the places for the long, hot Florida summer months. West and her assistants rolled up rugs, took down draperies and, for safekeeping, stored art, antiques, and other valuables in air-conditioned bank vaults. Everything left in the house would be wrapped like pastries in creosote paper to keep bugs away.[3] Before the owner returned the next winter, the house would be cleaned and put back in order. Groceries would be stocked, flowers arranged. Mabel and her crew would even change lightbulbs.

Along the way, Polly and John learned never to use a design twice. To own a sofa upholstered in the same fabric as your neighbor's was considered as much of a gaffe as showing up at a party in the same dress. Everything was supposed to be customized, although standards of good taste ensured that the differences would be minimal.

Notebooks, not unlike the ones hostesses kept of their favorite table settings, were created for regular clients. The journals held an array of photos, schematic drawings, furniture plans, model numbers, notes, and textile fragments, all dated and marked with pertinent information. Everything was on hand in case a replica of the same room in another house was desired, or something needed to be re-covered in the same fabric in the future. As with table-setting books, the detailed record prevented inadvertent duplication and was cross-indexed by date of purchase, model number, and client's name.

By the late 1930s, Polly and John were a success by their own estimation. "Our workroom was the top workroom," Polly recalled proudly. Every house owner in the area had been a customer for something at some point. "We haven't done everything [in Palm Beach], but we've been involved in it," said Polly.

In 1938, Polly contributed to *Katch's Kitchen*, a fundraising cookbook. Reprinted three times and sold nationally, the recipes were extolled by Eleanor Roosevelt in one of her "My Day" columns. Polly's sautéed veal kidneys were a stylish Depression-era dish, described in *Vogue* as classically French and perfect for serving at intimate suppers. Maitland Belknap, who worked as a designer for Jessup Inc. in the 1930s, provided a recipe for a wine-soaked orange chicken. ("The Delano sauterne is good and costs 59 cents a bottle," he wrote.)

Fig. 20
John (holding a Whitman's Sampler box of chocolates) and Polly Jessup. They look so comfortable that this photo may have been taken in their house at 922 Paseo Palmera, West Palm Beach, where they lived from 1930 to 1945. John turned sixty in 1936, Polly thirty-five. The man with the glasses is unknown. Courtesy of the Daniel Family, PFPB.

Top Hat and Tails

During the 1930s and early '40s, John and Polly joined the Palm Beach social scene, attending charity balls, giving dinners, and putting in regular appearances at the Everglades Club and the Bath & Tennis Club. Socializing helped their bottom line. Addison Mizner called his dinner jacket his "fishing clothes," a quip the Jessups may have appreciated.

In the days before Prohibition ended, Polly would buy a cake (chocolate or coconut), then she and John would head to the Royal Poinciana Hotel where cocktails were served in teacups. The cake was a winking cover for the "tea party." Dinners might be at Bradley's Beach Club, the private gambling house and restaurant, where their favorite dish was pompano poached in champagne. On one occasion, the chef gave Polly a treasured recipe for mustard sauce. Recalling the long-gone Palm Beach institution in her eighties, Polly enthused: "Oh, we loved Bradley's. There has been nothing ever as good, has there? Those green carpets and that white wicker furniture."

Resorts thrived on card games and sports, and John was a regular in local golf, bridge, and backgammon tournaments. The sportswriter Elon Jessup, John's younger brother, had published *Intimate Golf Talks*, a popular guide to the pastime. The book enhanced John's standing as an authority on the game; in 1937, he was appointed a West Palm Beach golf commissioner.

Going out helped the Jessups keep abreast of real estate transactions, marriages, and divorces. In Dominick Dunne's 1989 satirical novel, *People Like Us*, a Sister Parish-like decorator is unpleasantly surprised to hear gossip about a couple's separation: "'It can't be true,' cried Cora, slamming down her iced tea glass on the table with such force that diners at the next table stared. The specter of a lost account loomed. 'I'm making new slipcovers for their dining room chairs in Locust Valley!'" (fig. 20).

War

Palm Beach began to transform the moment war was declared on December 10, 1941. The military established bases there, and the sudden influx of servicemen and women turned the fashionable winter spot into a year-round community. The Biltmore Hotel was converted into a Coast Guard training center for women; the Breakers Hotel into a 500-bed army hospital. Frederick and Amy Guest donated their winter residence, Villa Artemis, to the navy as a place for officers to convalesce. Private yachts like Edsel Ford's were requisitioned. Joseph and Permelia Reed closed down the hotel part of the Jupiter Island

Fig. 21
The blue linen and red cap uniforms of Palm Beach's Volunteers for Victory (Polly Jessup, right). Courtesy of the Daniel Family, PFPB.

Club at the beginning of the war, not realizing the demand for a stateside vacation would grow higher once overseas travel was banned for civilians.

Jessup Inc. somehow managed to stay afloat during World War II. Days after war was declared, the party-loving Wolcott Blairs sold their sumptuous oceanside house to a dour couple, Alfred P. and Irene Sloan. Known as Silent Sloan, Alfred was chairman of General Motors. Jessup Inc. created furniture for the couple, and Polly likely helped them decorate. These kinds of commissions became increasingly rare.

For interior designers, times were tough. Metal, wood, and even goose down were needed by the government. Skilled labor was scarce, and the company constantly advertised for cabinetmakers, seamstresses, and upholsterers. They drew from their own lumber stock. In 1942 they still had mahogany, birch, cherry, pine, and cypress available. By the end of the war, bamboo was the predominant material for the increasingly rare custom-made furniture commission.

Polly joined the Canteen Corps of Volunteers for Victory, which served food and drink to enlisted men. She cooked seven days a week, making huge pots of potato salad, soups, sandwiches, ice cream, and pie. Later in life, she said that the "boys" loved her kidney stew. The Reeds lent their French chef to the officer's club on Hobe Sound. He made aspics and other finicky dishes, but, to the amusement of Polly, the officers weren't impressed. Polly laughed, "They wanted a roast beef sandwich or a little ham and eggs or something like that" (fig. 21).

War did not change John's life as much as his wife's. Too old to enlist, he played golf often at the Everglades Club and in weekly backgammon tournaments. Architect Maurice Fatio died in December 1943, and John was an executor of the complicated estate, which was settled two years later. John was not alive to witness the final court motion.

On May 23, 1945, John died at home of liver cancer linked to cirrhosis. Although the front-page obituary in *The Palm Beach Post* says he passed away after a short illness, his death was obviously not sudden. In 1941, Polly had successfully sued to remove the laws of coverture that prevented her, as a married woman, from signing contracts. On April 1, 1945, John attended a dinner at the Everglades Club. By the end of that month, the company held a fire sale of the furnishings from the Via Parigi showroom.

Throughout her life, Polly was known for her self-possession and serenity. John's death unsettled her. She refused to return to the house where he had died. Polly's attitude so alarmed employees that they moved her possessions to an apartment at 444 Chilean Street without her help. By the end of the year she seemed to have settled into her new role as sole owner of Jessup Inc. and was stable enough to co-chair the Worth Avenue Christmas decoration committee with her friend, the interior designer Anne Lanfranchi.

Postwar Years

After the war, Jessup Inc. was one of the last interior design companies in Florida to make its own furniture, which was so sturdy that the joke was that if Palm Beach were hit by an earthquake, the house might fall down but the Jessup Inc. chairs would still be standing.

Projects were finished (carved, stained, and glazed), passed onto a painter for decoration, or sent to the upholstery shop. The upholstery shop employed a dozen or so. Cushions were stuffed to order. One hundred percent down was used for the arms and back. Foam was used as a core of the seat, which was then wrapped in down. The upholsterers sewed muslin onto the article and did their own cutting. No staples were ever used. Everything was lined and interlined. Most work was custom, but the muslin on stock pieces was overlaid with tan sateen (which could be cleaned if it was in storage for any length of time).

The meticulous attention lavished on each commission was not always apparent at first glance. If a wall or a piece of furniture looked white, close observation disclosed a pale, colored wash. Interior designer Mimi Maddock McMakin said, "I can walk into a house and immediately spot a Jessup piece just by the way it's upholstered, the details. All furniture was marked with an inventory number that began with a 'B' so that you turned over the piece and could see the purchase order number and track it."

Pre- and postwar, Jessup Inc. specialized in comfort. "Make sure they have a bed, a chair, and a table," Polly advised her protégé Bermudes. "You would not believe how often that does not happen." Custom-made beds were scaled to the room, pink linings added inside lamp shades, drawers were fitted with hand-made Italian papers, and lazy Susans installed in cabinets to increase storage capacity.

Furnishing conventions shifted, reflecting changes in the way people lived. Chaise longues, for example, became more popular outdoors than in boudoirs. Furniture designs kept up with technology. Stereo and television cabinets supplanted radio casings. Built-in bars required icemakers as well as sinks and refrigerators.

In response to the postwar economy, Polly took on more staff than ever before. Shipping and receiving became a special department with four in delivery. More house openers were hired. Jobs became more specialized. One man's sole occupation was hanging curtains. As the numbers of people working for her expanded, Polly improved the working conditions. More bathrooms were added in 1950, and she began air-conditioning the plant in 1957.

As part of the expansion, Polly established an ancillary New York arm of Jessup Inc. at 120 East 55th Street. By the 1980s, the office had moved to two floors at 407 East 58th Street. The second-floor apartment was large enough for visiting Palm Beach Jessup Inc. employees to stay overnight. Hattie Van Gol served as the office manager. The income generated from Jessup Inc. was steady enough that, from 1947 to the 1980s, Polly rented an apartment for herself and would spend part of every month there.

The New York presence helped spread the word about Jessup Inc. Designers such as Eleanor McMillen Brown, Sister Parish, and Billy Baldwin placed commissions with the firm, as did architects Wyeth, Kemp Caler, Byron Simonson, and John Volk. The furniture plans at the Preservation Foundation contain a slew of New York specialty shops and furniture designers including Pamela Churchill (Mrs. Winston Churchill, later Harriman), Josephine Howell, Ginsburg & Levy, Tommi Parzinger, John Mascheroni, and Smith & Watson.

A Change in Style

Conservative design schemes began to eclipse Polly's earlier forays into Art Deco and modernism. The late 1950s and early 1960s was an era of stylized historicism exemplified by Cecil Beaton's set designs for *My Fair Lady*, Walt Disney's *Sleeping Beauty*, Jackie Kennedy's White House "restoration," and the extravagant draperies of British interior designer John Fowler for the houses of the British National Trust. Curtain patterns from Jessup Inc. became more fanciful and lavish, with tassels, cording, and shaped valances (fig. 22).

The well-heeled of Palm Beach retreated from the social revolutions of the late 1960s into their private clubs and homes. Restrictions increased. Style ossified. Polly was in her seventies, as were many of her clients. Her company catered discreetly to the upper crust, who craved modernization without change. Polly told the young interior designer Anne Pepper, "If your client wants a pink room and you feel very strongly it should be blue, you give them the best pink room you can. They, not you, have to live in it."

Jessup Inc. continued to prosper. Jayne Wrightsman engaged Jessup Inc. to help in a tireless quest to improve Blythedunes, the Wrightsman Palm Beach spread. Pamela Harriman employed the firm to spruce up her

Fig. 22
Polly in the downstairs drafting room of her Phipps Plaza house with the designer Carl Bretz. The window curtain fabric was a reproduction of an eighteenth-century indigo resist print and may have been supplied by Zina Akintievsky, a New York–based Russian immigrant who sold hand-blocked textiles. Akintievsky provided the reproduction fabric for the Whitby Hall period rooms that Polly and Bretz collaborated on in 1956 at the Detroit Institute of Arts. The Society of the Four Arts, Gioconda and Joseph King Library Collection.

Hobe Sound beach house and Middleburg, Virginia, estate. Diana Strawbridge Wister, a Campbell's Soup heiress, used the Jessup Inc. for her place in Palm Beach, as did the fox hunter and topiary enthusiast, Harvey Ladew, in Gulf Stream. Commissions were accepted from clients in conservative communities across the country (Seal Harbor, Maine; Lookout Mountain, Tennessee; Scottsdale, Arizona; Easthampton, New York; Grosse Pointe, Michigan).

The style revolution of the 1980s shocked Polly. Unapologetic glamor supplanted whispering good taste. The change was personified by the new president, former Hollywood star and California governor Ronald Reagan and his wife, Nancy. At the beginning of her husband's first term, the First Lady proudly announced her order for 220 new White House place settings, which she had designed with double rings of gold and "Nancy Red" rims. That same day, her husband slashed the budget for subsidized school lunches and allowed ketchup to count as a vegetable. A scarlet-colored scandal erupted, dominating the papers for weeks. Some blamed it all on Nancy's deliberate sidelining of the White House Fine Arts Committee. The Committee, which dated to the Kennedy era, had become self-inflated guardians of good taste. One member, Pamela Cunningham Copeland, complained, "If she [Nancy] hadn't ignored us, her White House china problems would never have happened. We would have quietly paid for it and made it available for her use. There would have been no publicity."[4] Scandal, which always involved a violation of accepted standards, was, ipso facto, in bad taste. But as Copeland and her WASP colleagues learned, accusing someone of lacking in taste was a flaccid weapon without power to punish. Good taste as a social cudgel was history (fig. 23).

A new Gilded Age, the second that Polly lived through, had begun. Obvious opulence became the accepted norm. Twenty-two-carat gold leaf was applied with abandon on everything from ceiling cornices to desserts. Old rules crumbled. Thick, bullion-fringe curtains puddled on the floor. Patterned wallpaper, which Polly once used solely in the bathroom, lined the walls of trendsetting drawing rooms. During the first Christmas season of the Reagan administration, a new maxim swept the country, which first appeared in a Palm Beach needlework shop on a pillow: "Nouveau is Better than No Riche at All."

The look of Old Money was why customers hired Jessup Inc. The young Fanjuls became patrons, as did Canadian publisher Conrad Black. McGinnis tended to these new clients. Some of them paid in cash, which worried Polly. "You have the Mellons, and we have the felons," McMakin teased, years before Black went to prison for mail fraud and obstruction of justice.

Polly coped by employing young designers unfazed by the skyrocketing prices for custom work. When novelist Dominick Dunne wrote *People Like Us* in the 1980s, he included a scene intended to appall the reader: a decorator computed the curtain budget by multiplying the number of windows by seven thousand. It was a new and not necessarily pleasant world for Polly.

Fig. 23
Polly dressed for an evening out in Palm Beach: lipstick, hair swept back from her face, silk dress, glittering velvet purse, and pearls with a lapis lazuli clasp around her neck, circa 1985. Courtesy of the Daniel Family, PFPB.

In her oral history at the Historical Society, Polly thought back about what the town was like when she first arrived: "Nobody could have imagined that Palm Beach would become what it has become . . . banks and expensive clothes and jewels." The growing inequality between rich and poor made her mourn for the paternalism of the past: "The doctors that took care of the Vanderbilts in the winter, took care of the poor for free in the summer. And we would meet in the Everglades Club . . ."

In 1985, Donald Trump and his wife Ivana bought Mar-a-Lago. Polly had been to Mar-a-Lago many times, as a professional and also as a guest of the original owner, Marjorie Merriweather Post. Time had softened the estate's theatrical glare, but the Trumps wanted to restore the glitter. They asked Polly, somewhat misguidedly, to help. Polly always gave people the benefit of the doubt, and she assured her dubious staff that the Trumps would be lovely. Polly was accompanied by McGinnis and his assistant, Lois Wideman.

To Polly's surprise, a cultural clash erupted between her and the triumphant new owners of Mar-a-Lago. The Trumps received Polly in the master bedroom. Ivana was sprawled across the bed horizontally, flicking through a magazine. She didn't acknowledge the prospective design team. Though Polly said she knew Mar-a-Lago well, Donald insisted she and her team take a tour. On their return to the bedroom, Ivana was sorting through Post's heavily embroidered bed linens. Perched on a bench at the end of the bed, Donald asked the exhausted eighty-six-year-old Polly: "Now that you have seen how tired this place is, how about a deal?" Snapping to attention, Ivana announced her own list of demands. "We want a discount," she said. "My people will order all the fabric wholesale and do all the work." And whatever her staff couldn't do, Jessup Inc. would. And Ivana would have first priority in the workshops.

Wideman stood behind Polly. She knew that when her boss got upset, her face remained impassive but her back twitched uncontrollably. As Ivana spoke, the flowers on the back of Polly's silk dress were in motion. After Ivana finished, there was a long pause. Polly finally spoke, "Mr. and Mrs. Trump," she said. Her face and voice were measured and grave. "Jessup Inc. does not cut deals."

She turned to her flabbergasted staff and said, "Come along, Lambies."

Notes

1. "Lark" is a word that twentieth-century women designers often used when explaining why they were in a money-making business.
2. J. Wadsworth Travers, *Beautiful Palm Beach,* 1929; Emelie Keyes, "Two Hundred Years in Ten Minutes is the Record Being Made by Jessup," *The Palm Beach Post,* September 13, 1931.
3. Thanks to Hank Cochran for providing information.
4. Interview with Copeland prior to 2001, Preservation Foundation of Palm Beach.

NOTABLE CLIENTS AND THEIR JESSUP INC. ROOMS

Unlike her contemporaries, Syrie Maugham and Dorothy Draper, Polly was not selling an identifiable look. The hallmarks of Jessup Inc. were broader: comfortable, high-quality furniture, logical groupings, and fastidious window coverings. Her firm sold perceptible good taste, variations of which included both modern and conservative styles.

Louis and Irma Levy, Palm Beach, 1934

The earliest known photographs of interiors by Jessup Inc. were taken at this house which Addison Mizner built for himself in 1919. He sold it almost immediately to Harold ("Mike") Vanderbilt, who asked him to enlarge it. Vanderbilt lived there only a few years before getting entangled in an unpleasant legal dispute with his neighbors, Alfred and Elizabeth Kay. He lost in court, and the 1928 hurricane caused more headaches, spurring Vanderbilt to commission another house. By 1930, he had abandoned El Solano.

Four years later, Vanderbilt sold his home to the New York lawyer Louis Sampter Levy and his wife, Irma. The Levys had been coming to Palm Beach since 1919. Louis, more showbiz than the usual Jessup Inc. client, represented the art dealer Lord Duveen as well as Lillian Gish and Florenz Ziegfeld. After Levy was disbarred for corruption in the state of New York in 1939, he and his wife moved to Palm Beach to live full time.

The severe forms of the Levys' Art Deco collection contrasted with Mizner's romantic architectural backdrop, making El Solano unique in the Jessup Inc. oeuvre. The dining room walls were originally half-paneled in Woodite, the upper portion painted with an outdoor market scene. By 1934, the wainscoting was replaced with white leather and the images of villagers with Spanish galleons.

The table was ornamented with three crystal trays by Jean Luce of Paris (used for a seashell display). Luce may have also done the white-enameled, U-shaped, rectangular-based candlesticks. The dining room screen that hid the butler's preparations was white leather, and the floors were covered in shaved hide. These Syrie Maugham–like flourishes seem appropriate, as the white leather chairs around the table were her design.[1] Three years earlier, Maugham had used them for the first time in the well-publicized Palm Beach dining room of Harrison and Mona Williams. Were the Levys' chairs bought from Maugham? Could Jessup Inc. have made the chairs for Maugham and then Polly used the design for the Levys? Or was Polly copying Maugham at the request of the client? It should be noted that Polly used identical chairs in her office at the Georgia Avenue factory (fig. 24).

Ernest and Josephine Kanzler, Hobe Sound, 1933–39

The Jessups accepted all jobs, regardless of size. The drawings from their furniture shop show orders for picture frames and flower boxes as well as four-poster beds and dining room tables. Their humility paid off. One of their most significant business relationships began with a commission to silence the lid of a clothing hamper. Polly, having been summoned by Ernest and Josephine Kanzler to listen to the offending sound, assured the aggrieved couple that a strip of felt lining could solve the problem. It did. A commission for a bridge table followed. In 1939,

Fig. 24
Art Deco dining room at Louis and Irma Levy's house, El Solano. The nailhead-trimmed white leather chairs were identical to the ones Syrie Maugham used in the dining room at the Harrison Williams house three years earlier. Photograph by Harlow D. Gaines. The Society of the Four Arts, Gioconda and Joseph King Library Collection.

the Kanzlers hired Jessup Inc. to decorate their new Henry Corse-designed Hobe Sound house and then, over time, their other residences in Seal Harbor, Maine, and Grosse Pointe, Michigan. Josephine's sister, Eleanor Ford, wife of Edsel, followed suit; so did their cousin, art collector Robert Hudson Tannahill, at least one of the Kanzler children, all four of the Fords' children, and some of the grandchildren. The hamper lid fix resulted in decades of work for Jessup Inc. (fig. 25).

Joseph Verner and Permelia Reed, Hobe Sound, 1934

In 1933, a thirty-one-year-old Yalie named Joseph Verner Reed bought the real estate of the languishing Olympia-Picture City project from the Drexel Biddle family. Reed and his wife Permelia wanted to create a winter island retreat for themselves, their friends, and their friends' friends in the style of the members-only community of Tuxedo Park. Even before the Reeds moved into their house on Hobe Sound, the most genteel and gentile of Florida resorts became Jessup Inc.'s turf. According to

Fig. 25
The Kanzlers' living room, designed by Jessup Inc., was more formal than the usual Hobe Sound retreat. The chintz was gray, yellow, jade, and white, with gray carpet and bleached floors. The yellow raw silk curtains go all the way to the alcove ceiling, adding height to the room, while the horizontal slats of the venetian blinds add width. The furniture arrangement was meant to foster conversation, but, according to visitors, the Kanzlers' poker-faced English butler increased the room's froideur. Photograph by Peter A. Nyholm, late 1930s. The Society of the Four Arts, Gioconda and Joseph King Library Collection.

Polly, John tested the water for the proposed development. In 1934, while the Reeds' house on Hobe Sound (which they called Villa Artemis, after the gods and goddesses theme of Olympia) was being remodeled by New York architect Henry Corse, Joseph stayed with the Jessups in Palm Beach.

Corse and Polly teamed up to renovate the old Olympia Inn for the Reeds, who wanted to make it into a clubhouse. Polly collaborated with Palm Beach designer Anne Lanfranchi on revamping what the Reeds planned to call the Jupiter Island Club, which consisted of cottages surrounding two clubhouses, one on the ocean side. When the oceanside Beach Club burned down in 1938, Polly and Lanfranchi spiffed it back up with light gray paint, primrose cushions, and indigo blue umbrellas. Not everyone was impressed. On reviewing the Club, a Chicago gossip columnist expressed surprise at the lack of "chi-chi." Permelia gloated at the critique. Old money simplicity, dowdy enough to repel the nouveaux riches, was exactly what she intended.

In the late winter of 1945, artist Walt Kuhn wrote about the rarefied life on the island in a series of letters now in the Smithsonian Archives. Kuhn was on the island to paint portraits and spent time with Mary Conover (Minna) Mellon, the first wife of Paul, the philanthropist and heir to the Pittsburgh banking fortune, who was in Europe serving with the OSS. Kuhn was taken by surprise by her security staff: "Minna has a plain clothes man on hand always. Fear of kidnapping and robbery as she's all alone. What a life!" Polly decorated the Mellon house, which Kuhn described as

Fig. 26
Dark floors covered with cream-colored rugs anchor the Hamm living room, which with the pale upholstery, mirrored walls, and abundance of windows was as airy as a cream puff. The foliage painting in the back may have been by the artist Henry LaCagnina, who painted the murals and screens for Polly when she decorated the dining room at the Palm Beach Bath & Tennis Club in 1939. Photograph by Frank Turgeon, circa 1937. The Society of the Four Arts, Gioconda and Joseph King Library Collection.

"beautifully appointed but strenuously simple and fitted for the tropics, everything is white and practically all the furniture is bamboo. A Spanish butler, Luis, and trim white maids in black uniforms." Simplicity was relative.

More than anyone else, Permelia was responsible for institutionalizing bigotry on the island. Unapologetically antisemitic with a flaring temper, she was feared by friends and enemies who called her "The Queen." Polly was Permelia's interior designer for decades, in Hobe Sound and Greenwich. One reason Polly remained in Permelia's good graces was that she refused to be baited. In response to one of Permelia's angry outbursts, Polly responded evenly, "Why Permelia, we have known each other since we were girls." Privately, Polly agreed that Permelia's obsession with the unpretentious bordered on the absurd. Polly joked that her clients on Hobe Sound wanted to cover gold bathroom faucets with birch bark. An outsider could easily be fooled, as they were meant to, by the seemingly plain surfaces.

William Hamm Jr., Hobe Sound, 1937

William Hamm Jr.'s penchant for streamlined design is reflected in this contemporary decor. Hamm, the scion of a wealthy St. Paul Minnesota beer manufacturer, was kidnapped in 1933. Ransomed and released physically unharmed, he became extremely wary and avoided publicity for the rest of his life. These rare photos of the interior of his beach house were not published in his lifetime for reasons of security (fig. 26).

Gladys McCormick-Goodhart, Hobe Sound, 1937

Gladys McCormick-Goodhart was the English-born, divorced wife of the International Harvester heir Frederick McCormick-Goodhart. The room Polly created for Gladys was in the summer mode of a British country house, with straw-matted floors, chintz slipcovered seating, and dark wood furniture. Although the McCormick-Goodhart room was traditional and Hamm's modern, the arrangement was almost the same (fig. 27).

Edsel and Eleanor Ford, Hobe Sound, 1937

In 1937, the Reeds sold some of their Hobe Sound property to Edsel and Eleanor Ford. The Fords were immediately besieged by decorators offering their services: Martin Becker of Alavoine of New York and Paris, Ben Worrell of his eponymous Palm Beach store, and Polly, none of whom were hired. Instead, the Fords

"The supreme excellence is simplicity."

Edith Wharton and Ogden Codman Jr., *The Decoration of Houses*, 1897

made the unconventional choice to build a dock on their new property and live on their yacht, the *Onika*, the interior of which had been done five years earlier by Carlhian of Paris. They hired Jessup Inc. to spruce up the French design company's Chippendale-ish rooms with paint and new upholstery. The Fords also built a one-story structure (living room, dressing rooms, and kitchen—no bedrooms) where they could entertain onshore. For this project, the Fords hired the industrial designer Walter

Fig. 27
In the McCormick-Goodhart living room, the slipcovers and curtains may have been made from an *indienne* from Brunschwig & Fils, one of Polly's favorite fabric sources. The chinoiserie design features waving palms, lobed medallions, and Chinese figures under umbrellas. Photograph by Frank Turgeon, circa 1937. The Society of the Four Arts, Gioconda and Joseph King Library Collection.

Teague, who had done the Art Deco rooms in the Fords' Grosse Pointe house. The aluminum, bleached wood, and leather furnishings, some of which had to be shipped from France, cost over $39,000. Polly's contribution: a few dark blue leather cushions made in her shop. While this assignment may have been disappointing, it was the start of a relationship with the Fords that would grow over time.

Edsel and Eleanor Ford, Grosse Pointe, before World War II

The Fords rejected the Palm Beach firm for their Florida house but began to consult Polly for help at their main residence in Grosse Pointe, Michigan. Polly sold over $45,000 worth of goods to the couple for this house in 1941. The miscellaneous items included a custom-made chaise longue in tan sateen for a guest room, a reproduction Louis XV bed with mattress and box spring for the former bedroom of the governess, and quite a few antique bibelots.

Fig. 28
A lacy guest room design by Jessup Inc. for the Fords' Grosse Pointe house. For the middle class, style choices tended to be oppositional: either modern or traditional. The rich had more real estate, so they didn't have to choose. Bars, card rooms, and second (or third or fourth) homes were often modern, while primary residences, particularly the living rooms and bedrooms, were more likely to be traditional. Courtesy of the Edsel & Eleanor Ford House.

Fig. 29
The oversized pair of octagonal mirrors in Jesse Shaughnessy's dining room, which reflect light from the windows on the opposite side of the room, were inset deeply enough to hold a vase of flowers. The sheen and gloss of this light-hearted Chinese Chippendale room was very different from the dark and sober historicist fiction of the McAneeny dining room ten years before. Photo by Samuel Gottscho. PFPB.

The new curtains for the master bedroom cost $2,192, just slightly more than the pair of eighteenth-century Louis XV ormolu candlesticks ($2,000) for the drawing room. Polly would work with Eleanor on this house for the next thirty-five years (fig. 28).

Jesse Shaughnessy, Palm Beach, 1938

The Jessups hobnobbed frequently with Francis A. Shaughnessy, president of the First National Bank of Palm Beach, the first commission of Jessup Inc. In 1936, Shaughnessy died. Two years later, his fifty-two-year-old widow, Jesse, enlisted the Jessups to help furnish and decorate her new Wyeth-designed house on South Ocean Boulevard. Just before the war, in 1941, Jesse married Edward F. Swenson, and Polly redecorated for them. Estée Lauder bought the house in 1964, and Polly, who no doubt knew the house inside out, redecorated the place a third time (fig. 29).

Carll Tucker, Hobe Sound, 1941

Carll Tucker employed Polly to furnish this Art Deco house, which had been designed by Henry Corse. Corse, like Polly, rejected a defining style for his firm. In her 1978 pamphlet *A Kaleidoscope of Jupiter Island*, Permelia Reed

Fig. 30
The symmetrical vases in the back of the Tucker dining room were used as focal points, like the mirrors in the Shaughnessy house. Note the servant call bell wired into the table end. Photo by Samuel Gottscho, 1941. The Society of the Four Arts, Gioconda and Joseph King Library Collection.

Fig. 31
Leather benches by Jessup Inc. at the opening of the Norton Gallery and School of Art, 1941. Photograph by Frank Turgeon. PFPB.

wrote that Corse was responsible for twenty-one houses on the island: "The amazing fact is that they are all very different" (fig. 30).

Norton Gallery and School of Art, Palm Beach, 1941

After Polly finished designing the home of Ralph and Elizabeth Norton, the art collecting couple asked her to work on the interiors of the museum they proposed to open. The crisp lines of the benches in the gallery were designed by the Jessup Inc. cabinetmaker Joseph F. Weber and made in the workshops on Georgia Avenue (fig. 31).

Worthington and Marion Margery Scranton, Hobe Sound, 1942

One whole-house commission Jessup Inc. completed after Pearl Harbor was for Worthington and Marion Margery Scranton on Hobe Sound. Scranton and his wife—called "The Duchess" by friends (and probably enemies, too, with a different inflection)—lived most of the year in the central Pennsylvania city named for his grandfather. The Duchess, a former suffragette, was a leader in the Republican party. (Their son, William, was elected governor in 1963. He credited his mother with getting him into politics.)

The Scrantons' Hobe Sound house was said to have been inspired by Hawaiian design. The house was U-shaped, enclosing a patio from the wind. One of Jessup Inc.'s most publicized works, the house appeared in *Architectural Forum* (September 1944), *House Beautiful* (April 1945), and *Vogue* (November 15, 1948). Only *House Beautiful* credited Jessup Inc. (fig. 32).

Fig. 32

The mismatched furniture in the Scranton house reflected the WASP abhorrence for anything that looked too new. Polly understood that eclecticism was a virtue in the recently built beach house, which had two master bedrooms and a service wing that included sleeping quarters for live-in help. Photograph by Samuel Gottscho, 1942. PFPB.

Fig. 33
Jessup Inc. seldom took commercial work, but an exception was made for Catherine "Tat" Saunders, whom Polly and John knew through the Worth Avenue Merchants Association. For the Palm Beach location of Saunders's eponymous clothing store, a drawing-room-like area was created for customers, circa 1944. Marion Sims Wyeth was the architect of the building. PFPB.

Catherine "Tat" Saunders, Palm Beach, 1944
Tat Saunders was a clothing shop owned by two sisters, Catherine ("Tat") and Mary. Resort wear was their specialty. They were successful enough to have branches in Palm Beach, New York, Boston, and other places (fig. 33).

Hugh and Edith Kirkland, Palm Beach, 1944–45
Billy Baldwin, called the "dean of interior designers" in his 1983 *New York Times* obituary, loved Palm Beach. After he was discharged from the defense work he was doing in Florida during World War II, he decided to stay in the state. "Palm Beach was like a city being reborn. Everything was booming." He asked to join Polly's firm and was hired on the spot. He found her enchanting and her attention to detail amazing. Although his stay in Palm Beach was short, less than a year, he became a huge fan of his boss: "Polly Jessup's taste is simply beautiful. … Her extravagant insistence upon quality, and quality only, has never been equaled" (fig. 34).

Gerard and Grace Lambert, Manalapan, 1947
Gerard "Jerry" Lambert was an eccentric industrialist. Heir to a moribund company that made the mouthwash Listerine, he capitalized on the fear of bad breath (halitosis) to invent

Fig. 34
Timing suggests that Billy Baldwin may have had a hand in the spare, almost modern decor of the Kirkland house. The Society of the Four Arts, Gioconda and Joseph King Library Collection.

a million-dollar product category. After selling that company, he made Gillette razors into a cutting-edge phenomenon. At the end of World War II, he commissioned the architectural firm of Marion Sims Wyeth, a fellow Princetonian, to build an estate—a double house that he would later dub Gemini. His wife, Grace, desired an ocean view; he preferred a lakefront. Jerry's imaginative solution was to purchase a piece of land with frontage on both. To connect the two sides, which were split by a thirty-foot public road, he proposed a tunnel. In his autobiography, *All Out of Step*, Jerry joked that the wild idea propelled Wyeth into the hospital. Wyeth's

Fig. 35
The color blue united the bold patterns in the lakeside living room. A retractable wall separated the room from the outside pool, circa 1947. PFPB.

Fig. 36
Grace Lambert's living room at Gemini, which her husband described in his autobiography as "severely Greek." The decoration was likely by Virginia Johnson of Jessup Inc., who was the wife of the architect. Courtesy of PFPB.

partner, William R. Johnson, accepted the challenge. It took Johnson three years to work out the complex engineering and architecture of Gemini (figs. 35 and 36).

Each half of Gemini had its own living room, bedroom, dressing room, kitchen, heating plant, and staff of servants. Jerry's servants, headed by Thomas the butler, were Black, and Grace's white. The interiors of the houses also had distinct color schemes. Green predominated on her ocean half, while blue prevailed on the lakeside. They lived mostly on her side and used his (which had its own pool) for guests. The decoration was by Jessup Inc. (and perhaps Johnson's wife Virginia, then a vice president of the firm). Jerry's friend Noel Coward suggested that the tunnel also function as a music room. Lit at each end by skylights and warmed by a central fireplace, the music room, replete with an electric organ, became a popular party venue. Too popular: to the Lamberts' horror, Gemini turned tourist attraction. Jerry wrote, "They were not trippers or sightseers but the nicest people you could imagine. They came themselves and they brought their friends. We had no peace and no privacy. We found no way to be human and yet to repel them. These people would come early, drink cocktails, swim in the pool and stay on." By 1954, the Lamberts found the entertaining exhausting. They sold Gemini to Loel Guinness and his glamorous wife, Gloria. The day after the sale, Gerard saw Guinness, who looked pale. "He told me, with a strange look in his eyes, that at a big dinner the night before twenty people had asked if they could come and see the place. He asked me what he had got into. I told him he had got into what I had got out of."

Fig. 37
PIcassos adorn the Tannahill entrance hall. Courtesy of the Detroit Institute of Arts.

Robert Tannahill, Grosse Pointe, 1948
From 1947 to '48, Polly's attention was focused on the house of Robert Tannahill, the cousin of Eleanor Ford. Tannahill was more like a brother than a cousin to Ford and her sister Josephine Kanzler. The three grew up together, with their mothers, in the house of their uncle, Joseph L. Hudson, founder of the eponymous Detroit department store. They were a remarkably clannish family. Tannahill lived in Detroit with his aunt, the mother of Ford and Kanzler, until her death in 1944. He then moved to Grosse Pointe, near the homes of his cousins.

A quiet bachelor with deep pockets and an interest in paintings, Tannahill was advised by the Detroit Institute of Arts director William R. Valentiner and his housemate, the museum curator Perry Townsend Rathbone. Tannahill traveled to Europe with them. He learned to be an adventurous collector. In Berlin, he bought German Expressionist works off easels before they were dry. He was also influenced by Edith Halbert, the New York dealer who counseled Abby Aldrich Rockefeller, co-founder of the Museum of Modern Art. He bought folk art from Halbert and landscapes by Georgia O'Keefe, John Marin, and Charles Sheeler. By the time he commissioned his house in 1947, he owned a stellar group of modern European and American paintings, eighteenth-century French silver, African sculpture, Chinese porcelains, pre-Columbian textiles, and American antiques.

Fig. 38
Tannahill's second-floor sitting room, furnished with upholstered club chairs, American antiques, and curtains made from Scalamandré fabric. The painting above the fireplace surround is Robert de la Fresnaye's 1921 *Portrait of Jean-Louis Gambert*. Above the club chair is Georges Rouault's 1909 *Standing Nude*. Courtesy of the Detroit Institute of Arts.

When Polly decorated his house, she had to knit this eclectic assemblage into an organic whole. She hung two Picassos in the small, sparsely furnished entrance hall: *Head of a Harlequin* and *Bather by the Sea (Dora Maar)*. Another Picasso, the five-foot-high *Woman Seated in an Armchair*, was displayed on a wall in the stairwell. Tannahill called the enormous canvas "the mistress of the house," although the only extant photo shows the painting bathed in shadow (fig. 37).

At the end of the long process of decorating, Tannahill was so pleased that he asked Polly to help him on the new period rooms at the Detroit Institute of Arts, where he was honorary curator of American decorative arts. When Tannahill died in 1969, he left his $13 million collection and $12 million endowment to that institution. The size of the gift stimulated international interest and articles in *The Burlington Magazine* and *Apollo*. Fortunately, his collection was photographed before it was removed from the rooms. The description of his comfortable residence by *New York Times* art critic John Canaday read: "Mr. Tannahill's house gave no impression of being a collector's quarters, or even of being a rich man's domain, even though on the walls you found major paintings by (a partial list) Corot, Renoir, Degas, Van Gogh, Gaugin [*sic*], Seurat, Cezanne, Modigliani, Rouault, Klee, Matisse and Picasso." Polly must have been delighted (fig. 38).

Fig. 39
On the far right of the Abeggs' living room was Cézanne's *The Curtain* (today hung in a gallery at the Abegg-Stiftung museum). "Bruce" designed the sofa, covered in a cream-colored silk taffeta and the folding screen. Both are now in Villa Abegg. Courtesy of the Daniel Family, PFPB.

Fig. 40
The dramatically illuminated art in the Abeggs' New York dining room. A seventeenth-century bird's eye view of Venice attributed to Joseph Heintz the Younger dominated the room. Below the painting are two wooden sculptures of Moors (eighteenth or nineteenth century). Both works are now at the Villa Abegg in Switzerland. The disposition of the musician figures against the light-panel walls is unknown. The marble-topped table and chairs are part of the Abegg-Stiftung. Courtesy of the Daniel Family, PFPB.

Fig. 41
The modern-style living room of Clarence and Violet Prentice in their house at 911 Ocean Avenue in Delray Beach. Decoration by Virginia Johnson; architecture by Wm. Royster Johnson of Wyeth, King & Johnson; furniture by Jessup Inc., 1952. Courtesy of PFPB.

Fig. 42
Fresh air and louvered shutters took precedence over glass windows in the Jamaican getaway of Matthew and Jane Bartram Mellon. PFPB.

Werner and Peggy Abegg, New York City, 1951
Three months before the United States entered the war, Polly's sister Peggy married Werner Abegg, a Swiss millionaire. Abegg had left his family's Turin cotton manufacturing company in the hands of lawyers after Mussolini signed his pact with Germany. Newly arrived in the United States, he met Peggy. The couple shared a love of art, particularly ancient textiles. Their first address in New York was 121 East End Avenue, where Vincent Astor occupied the penthouse. In 1951 they moved to an even more exclusive address, One Sutton Place South. After a decade, they left the United States and moved to Europe. In Switzerland, they established the Abegg-Stiftung (Abegg Foundation), devoted to the conservation of historic textiles and art. Their nearby home, Villa Abegg, designed by F. Burrall Hoffman, of Paris and Hobe Sound, is now a museum (figs. 39 and 40).

Clarence and Violet Prentice, Delray Beach, 1952
Virginia Campbell Johnson, later Lady Christie (1909-2003), designed this room with her then-husband, William Royster Johnson, an architect in Marion Sims Wyeth's firm. In the 1940s, she was the vice president of Jessup Inc. but left in 1952 to open her own firm. She and Polly parted on good terms, and Virginia continued to order custom furniture at her former employer's workshops. In 1958, she divorced Johnson and married Sir Harold G. Christie, a wealthy Bahamian businessman whose role in the 1942 murder of his business partner, Sir Harry Oakes (a Jessup Inc. client), is still debated (fig. 41).

Matthew and Jane Bartram Mellon, Ocho Rios, Jamaica, 1955
John Volk, the architect, hired Italian craftsmen to build the house. The workmen were part of a small colony of British prisoners of war who

Fig. 43
Henry and Anne Ford's living room at Fordune. The Society of the Four Arts, Gioconda and Joseph King Library Collection.

had been interned on the island and decided to stay (fig. 42).

Henry and Anne Ford, Southampton, 1958
All four of Edsel and Eleanor's children became Jessup Inc. clients. The eldest son, Henry, and his wife Anne owned two houses in the 1950s: one in Southampton and the other in Grosse Pointe. Lacking the time to take on both projects, Polly steered the couple to the New York decorating firm McMillen Inc., which accepted the Grosse Pointe commission. Polly continued in an advisory role on the house and coordinated the acquisitions in Paris. Polly decorated the Southampton house, Fordune, by herself. Anne and Henry divorced in 1964, and Anne took sole ownership (figs. 43, 44, and 45).

Fig. 44
Jessup Inc. design for the curtains used in Henry and Anne Ford's living room. Courtesy of Anne Pepper, PFPB.

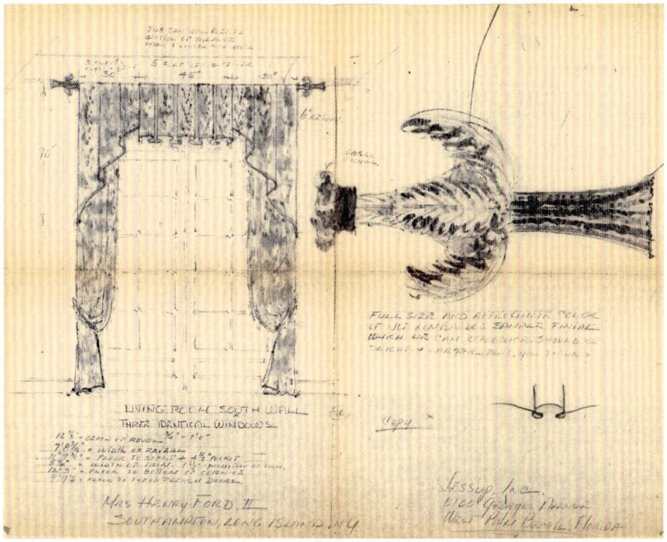

Fig. 45
Henry and Anne Ford's outdoor entertaining area, Southampton, 1958. The Society of the Four Arts, Gioconda and Joseph King Library Collection.

Fig. 46
The window valances evoked India in the bridge room and pool pavilion of Jessie Shaughnessy Swenson and her third husband, Edward F. Swenson. This was the second time Jessup Inc. worked in this Palm Beach house for Jessie. Photograph by Henry Fullerton. The Society of the Four Arts, Gioconda and Joseph King Library Collection.

Fig. 47
A shallow canopy bed for the Hobe Sound house of the Kennedy administration's Secretary of Treasury C. Douglas Dillon and his wife, Phyllis, circa 1962. The Francophile Dillon had served under Eisenhower as the American ambassador to France. Courtesy of Anne Pepper, PFPB.

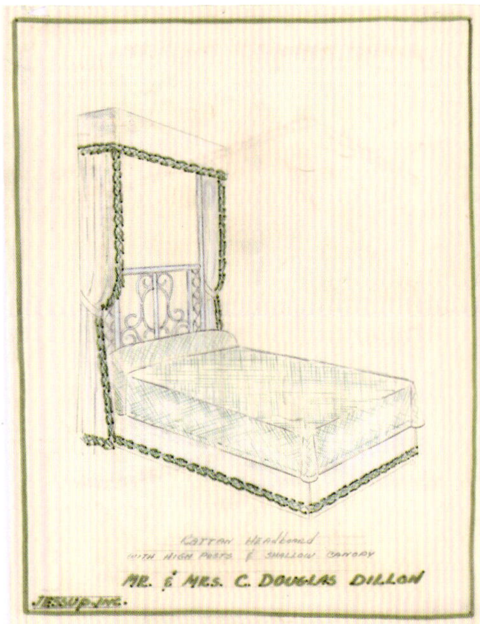

Jessie Shaughnessy Swenson and Edward F. Swenson, Palm Beach, 1960
The South Ocean Boulevard house of the Swensons was the site of many soirees. Only a year after they were married in 1941, her daughter Marie Bassett married his son Edward Jr. In 1960, Jessie Swenson was wheelchair bound but still ordering items from Jessup Inc. including bridge chairs, hence the assumed date of this bridge room. In 1964, the Swensons sold this house to Estée Lauder and moved to a house in Coral Gables that John Volk designed for them (fig. 46).

C. Douglas and Phyllis Dillon, Hobe Sound, 1962
Katharine Graham wrote in her memoirs that she thought Phyllis Dillon was the height of sophistication. Douglas served as the ambassador to France under Eisenhower but it was Phyllis who was presented in 1957 with the Legion of Honor by the French Prime minister. When the Dillons returned to the United States, Douglas was asked to join the Kennedy administration as Secretary of Treasury.
In October 1962, while her husband dealt with the deepening horror of the Cuban Missile Crisis, Phyllis ordered furniture for their Hobe Sound house from Jessup Inc. (fig. 47).

209 Phipps Plaza, Palm Beach, 1962
Polly moved into 209 Phipps Plaza in 1961. Volk and his artist wife Jane owned the single-family home and renovated it for her. She lived here for her final twenty-seven years (figs. 48, 49, and 50).

Fig. 48
Painted furniture and Bolognese painted panels in the entry hall of Polly Jessup's Phipps Plaza home. The panels seem to be from the same set that Polly installed at Henry and Anne Ford's Southampton house three years earlier. Courtesy of the Daniel Family, PFPB.

Fig. 49
Entrance to Henry and Anne Ford's home. The Society of the Four Arts, Gioconda and Joseph King Library Collection.

Fig. 50
Black-and-white photographs belie Polly's mastery of color. The subdued combinations of deep blue and moonlight in her living room evoke *l'heure bleue*, the French term for the blue hour of twilight when the sky and the earth are at the same level of luminosity. Between the two chairs in the foreground was a table covered in blue velvet, which gave emphasis to the blue velvet on the chair, a 1774 bergère signed by Pierre-Eloi Langlois. The painting over the mantle was by Wallace Herndon Smith, an American artist who was exhibited at the Society of the Four Arts in 1961, the same year Polly put her new home together. Courtesy of the Daniel Family, PFPB.

Fig. 51
The gleaming French-paneled drawing room in the Ford house. Polly's instructions about making it seem homelike seem to have been followed. Courtesy of the Edsel & Eleanor Ford House.

Alfonso and Alexandra Landa, Palm Beach, 1964

Alfonso Beaumont Brabourne Landa, known as Alfons, and his wife Alexandra Stefanopoulos, who was nicknamed Alexandra the Magnificent for her fundraising abilities, were prominent in Palm Beach society.

Edsel and Eleanor Ford's House as a museum, Grosse Pointe Shores, 1980

The Edsel and Eleanor Ford House was Polly's pièce de résistance. She began on the 30,000-square-foot Tudor Revival-style house while Edsel was still alive. After his death from stomach cancer in 1943, Eleanor and Polly became friends. They drew even closer following John Jessup's death in '45. Polly made Eleanor's house her pet project, fiddling with it for three decades. Paneling was added, fireplace mantles replaced, and furniture re-covered and restored to tip-top working order. In the Florida workshops of Jessup Inc., Eleanor's orders were always given priority. Eleanor died in 1976; four years later, the house was opened to the public as a museum. At the urging of Eleanor's children, Polly advised the curators on how to preserve the atmosphere of the home. The museum has the added distinction of being her only extant interior open to the public (figs. 51, 52, and 53).

During the final year of Polly's life, she recorded an interview with Edsel and Eleanor Ford House director James Bridenstine. She refused to sit down and, instead, wandered through the rooms. The director trailed behind

Fig. 52
Eleanor Ford's bedroom done in a Brunschwig et Fils floral. Courtesy of the Edsel & Eleanor Ford House.

Fig. 53
Detail of Eleanor Ford's bedroom. Courtesy of the Edsel & Eleanor Ford House.

her with docent John Hammell, who had the unenviable task of holding the microphone. They wanted Polly to reminisce; Polly wanted to get the house in order. The rooms should be alive, she said as she strode. To the consternation of Bridenstine and Hammell, Polly never stopped checking the lampshades and plumping the pillows. "The house needs to have the air of someone who cares," she said. She tutored them in the art of living well: leather looked better when it was a little worn; silver added sparkle to the dining room; little books should be scattered on bare tables; more and better flowers were needed everywhere. Politely dismissive of the bouquets already in place, she urged the befuddled Bridenstine to hire a Chicago florist, Medard Lange, who could instruct the volunteers on how Eleanor would have had her butler arrange the flowers.

Bridenstine tried to refocus Polly on some of his concerns. The two disagreed about the overlays to protect the carpets. Bridenstine preferred something dark, so dirt wouldn't show. "A little dirt won't matter," Polly said consolingly. She held out for a light color. Though she approved of the modern lamps ("You don't see them"), she pleaded against an institutional aesthetic: "Keep it shabby, the way it was." Above all, she told the two administrators not to worry so much and try to keep it looking lived-in: "Because it's an old—I mean, after all—it's the way the house was, isn't it?" Permelia Reed would approve.

JESSUP INC. EMPLOYEES

Good workmanship as distinct from designing, almost always commands a higher price than bad; and good artistic workmanship . . . [is even more] rare.

—Edith Wharton and Ogden Codman Jr., *The Decoration of Houses*

Prewar

Billy Baldwin (1903-1983) helped change American interior design by bringing in a classically based modernism. He worked with Polly before and after John's death. In his autobiography Baldwin wrote, "I had been offered a job by Mrs. John Jessup, who was a great friend [of his former employer, Ruby Ross Wood] and who made most of the curtains and slipcovers for her decorating jobs there. I had a terribly difficult evening with the Jessups trying to figure out a way to ask them if they would take me on. They were absolute angels, which they are, anyway, and I was given a job on the spot." John was apparently still alive when this occurred, perhaps late summer or early fall of 1944. Baldwin does not name the clients for whom he worked while he was with Jessup Inc. One possibility: Hugh and Edith Kirkland, who bought a completely furnished Palm Beach house in 1944 and had it redone by Jessup Inc. Photos of it appeared in the April 1945 issue of *Vogue* alongside a bedroom by Baldwin—his own at 155 Worth Avenue. Baldwin's Palm Beach bedroom changed his life. He wrote that the entire apartment was painted a "dark, shiny green, a revival of Elsie de Wolfe's famous green rooms. To let the painter know exactly what I had in mind, I had the audacity to give him as a sample a gardenia leaf that I had licked to glisten." Baldwin described his Palm Beach lair in detail, down to the sunflowers planted in the garden. Though he lasted only eighteen months with Jessup Inc., it was in Palm Beach that he discovered the power of dramatic color.

Maitland Belknap (1889-1958) arrived at Jessup Inc. as a designer after working at the Palm Beach offices of F. Burrall Hoffman Jr., Marion Sims Wyeth, Addison Mizner, Maurice Fatio, and Kemp Caler. With degrees in architecture from Princeton and Columbia, he helped Howard Major design Major Alley, and he lived there in one of Palm Beach's most picturesque houses. It's not clear when Belknap started at Jessup Inc., but he was employed there in the 1930s. In 1934, he and Polly remodeled the Jupiter Island Club's Beach House. In the collection of the Metropolitan Museum of Art there is a 1932-34 Walker Evans photograph of a ruffled chintz Palm Beach living room. This room, owned by Frederick and Norma Sears of Boston, appears in photos with others in the same house in the Jessup Inc. collection at the Society of the Four Arts. Notes on the photo at the Met describe the room as associated with Belknap. It's not clear how long he stayed at Jessup Inc. but by 1939 he had left. He taught classes on interior design at the Norton Gallery and School of Art.

Virginia Campbell Johnson (1909-2003). A Palm Beach native, in 1930 she married William Royster Johnson, an architect who would become a partner in Wyeth's firm. Sometime before 1941, Virginia joined Jessup Inc. as an interior decorator, and within six years was named vice president. Virginia, who specialized in Caribbean houses, left in 1952 to open her own design business. She continued to order custom furniture from her old employer. She divorced Johnson in 1958 and married Sir Harold G. Christie, a wealthy Bahamian businessman whose role in the 1942 murder of his business partner, Sir Harry Oakes (a Jessup Inc. client), is still debated. Virginia may have been responsible for the decoration at Westbourne, the house where Oakes was murdered.

Susanna "Sadie" Kort (1896-1984) was a long-time seamstress with Jessup Inc. who retired in 1968.

Joseph F. Weber (1903-1998) was born in Germany and started about the same time as Wilcox. Associated with the company for forty-eight years, he retired as chief cabinetmaker in 1978. In the 1970s, younger employees marveled at his house in West Palm Beach, which he bought during the Depression for $25.

Ray Wilcox (1888-1962) was one of the earliest employees at Jessup Inc. For twenty years he was the head cabinetmaker, retiring in the early 1950s.

Postwar

Skip Bermudes joined Jessup Inc. in the 1980s as an assistant to John Hulse. He and Polly (whom he and everyone else in the office always called Mrs. Jessup) spent many hours together. In her ninth decade, she rarely traveled solely. Skip drove her to appointments and accompanied her on her rounds. She rarely reminisced but often gave advice. She told Skip that that when Elsie de Wolfe was one of her subcontractors she explained to Polly that clients don't need a lot of choices. They need one plan—but it has to be the best.

Jack Braden (1921-1995), a Texan, was a designer and draftsman who worked in the New York office. On his travels to Europe, he sketched curtain designs, which he used as inspiration for his work.

Carl August Bretz (1904-1986) was an instructor of interior design at the Pennsylvania Museum School of Industrial Art before moving on to the New York office of Jansen. After being stationed in Jacksonville, Florida, during the war, he decided to stay in the state. Polly employed him in November 1945. He became foreman of the upholstery shop, and, in 1952, vice president of the company as a designer. He and Polly worked closely together for forty years.

Hank Brooks (1937-2024) started in the upholstery department in the fall of 1972. Carl Adams was the cigar-chomping foreman at that time. After Adams returned to his birthplace in North Carolina with mouth cancer, Brooks ran the workshop. When Jessup Inc. shut down in 1993, Brooks had been an employee for twenty-one years.

Henry Cochran was employed by Jessup Inc. after Polly Jessup died. As the last design assistant to John Hulse, he spent many hours sorting through the firm's papers. An architect by training, he continues to work with clients throughout the country, decorating and designing in the spirit of Jessup Inc.

John "Jack" Coon (1930-2020) joined Jessup Inc. in the early 1980s after a long campaign by the head of the woodshop, Eddie Thomas. Coon, who was not only a skilled cabinetmaker but a talented carver, had previously been a contractor. Coon left in 1988 and opened his own business. He rescued the old furniture plans from the trash bin when Jessup Inc. closed, and his daughter later donated the drawings to the Preservation Foundation of Palm Beach.

Dulce Fereira (1925-2017) was Jessup Inc.'s top embroiderer for twenty years or more. A formerly wealthy refugee from Cuba, she learned the art of fine sewing in her youth. She made lovely tufted ties in lieu of buttons, applied tiny flowers and minute-sized leaves onto upholstered headboards, and, for perfect bows on the backs of chairs, cut ties into the shape of spoons.

John Hulse (1917-1998), the artist, interior designer, and future owner of Jessup Inc., joined the company in 1971. A graduate of the Parsons School of Art in Paris, he worked with William Pahlmann at Lord & Taylor and later became head of Macy's Interior Design Department at a time when department stores were influential tastemakers. A painter whose work drew national attention, Hulse was entrusted with some of Polly's most prestigious accounts. In the 1980s, the rage for the English country look allowed him the freedom to imitate Old Masters to complete the "look." Among his clients were Estée Lauder in Palm Beach and John and Chan Mashek in Newport.

Hilda Stewart Martin (1910-2002) worked on and off at Jessup Inc. for a half century. Born in England, she was the reigning "dragon lady" of the purchasing department. Designers passed along orders to Hilda, who assigned them to the appropriate workshop. She was part of the upper staff at Jessup Inc. and ate lunch with Polly and the head designers in the company dining room. The dining room had its own cook and kitchen. Everyone else brought their lunch. She retired when the company closed in 1993.

Billy Mayhew (1922-1986) ran the curtain room at Jessup Inc. for decades.

Neal McGinnis (1924-2007) replaced Mimi in the Palm Beach office. Originally from North Carolina, McGinnis trained at Parsons after the war. Before coming to Jessup Inc., he worked as a window dresser in New York and designed theatrical sets on the weekends. Soon after arriving in the resort town, he was in a bar when a stranger introduced himself: "Hi, I'm Flanders Holland." McGinnis replied, "And I'm Paris, France." It was the beginning of a love affair that lasted the rest of their lives. Holland was a ballet teacher who later became the assistant director of the Norton Gallery and School of Art. The pair lived near the Ann Norton Sculpture Garden and were sought-after dinner guests. McGinnis's clients at Jessup Inc. included Conrad and Shirley Black, and Edgar and Bernice Garbisch.

Richard McKay was identified as a designer with Jessup Inc. (presumably in New York) in two articles, both of July 1965: "Found Space for Your Three-Dimensional Treasures" in House & Garden, which featured a wall of keys by McKay for New York artist Charles Rain, and Rita Reif's

Fig. 54
In this revealing 1967 portrait sketch by the artist Henry Koehler, Mimi Rand appears as pleased to model as Polly Jessup looks distressed. Courtesy of Skip Bermudes, PFPB.

piece "Cool Solutions" in the New York Times of July 6, 1965, which showed a drawing of a fabric-covered screen made by McKay for Anita Colby (1914-1992), a wealthy former film actress, author, and model who had a house in Oyster Bay, New York.

Anne Pepper joined Jessup Inc. New York in 1985 as a designer. Two years later, she moved to the Palm Beach office, where she assisted Neal McGinnis.

Mimi Rand (1905-1974) was the professional name of Emilie Bushnell Martin Durand Rand Lineaweaver, a much-married socialite with a side career in interior design. She hooked on with Polly in Palm Beach after the war. Polly shied away from anything that looked too fashionable, but Rand liked the frisson of fads. A glass aquarium table in her silver-and-chartreuse bedroom had been featured in a 1937 *Arts and Decoration* magazine. Polly made Mimi vice president in 1952. That year, Mimi married her fourth husband, Charles Pleasants Lineaweaver II. They moved to New York City. For the next twenty years, Mimi partnered with Polly on the 120 East 55th Street branch of Jessup Inc. In contrast to Polly, Mimi enjoyed publicity. *The New Yorker* ran a 1957 Talk of the Town "casual" on Mimi and her longtime interior decoration clients, Betsy and John Hay Whitney. An ornamental dinner table by Mimi was featured, along with creations by Billy Baldwin, Sister Parish, and Andy Warhol, in the 1960 book *Tiffany's Table Settings*. There were exhibitions of her watercolors and rooms in decorator showhouses. In the 1967 Wilderstein show, *Art & The Decorator*, Rand was the conduit for the majority of the paintings. She was credited with obtaining art from the collection of Carter Burdens, the Edgar Garbisches, and John Hay Whitney's sister and brother-in-law, Charles and Joan Payson—all of whom were in her social circle and client group. The outspoken Mimi would sometimes land work by exclaiming to friends, "What a mess! When are you going to redo this?" (fig. 54).

William P. "Robby" Robertson (1908-1983) replaced John as treasurer and spent his entire working life at the company. The designer Mimi Maddock McMakin remembered him as a charming man with a taste for mango daiquiris.

Nina Termina (1919-1997) started at Jessup Inc. in 1957 and retired in 1983. One of the senior staff, her sole job was to keep the solid woven fabric samples in order with current prices. Printed fabrics were kept elsewhere.

Edgar R. "Eddie" Thomas (1930-?). Welsh-born and partly raised in Great Britain, Thomas was only eighteen when he started at Jessup Inc. He was trained by Ray Wilcox and Joseph F. Weber. Thomas took over as shop foreman after Weber retired in 1978. Thomas always called Polly "Madam." Polly said he understood the construction of antique furniture almost intuitively. After disassembling a fake, he told her, "Madam, this doesn't smell right."

Marie "Mip" J. Vanderwaeren (1920-2001) was an interior designer in the New York office in the 1970s and '80s. Born in Belgium and a former airline hostess, her clients included Gladys Pulitzer Preston, whose husband was head of the World Bank.

Lois Wideman joined the company in the early 1970s as a draftsman but quickly moved into interior design and assisted John Hulse. She became a designer in her own right and left to work for herself.

Contract Employees

Margaret Caroline ("Sunny") Bippus is a Palm Beach native who became a model (1966 *Sports Illustrated* swimsuit cover) and designer. She worked with her friends Mimi McMakin and Carole Douglass as a contractor for Jessup Inc. (see "Color It Palm Beach," *House & Garden*, August 1983). She later opened her own firm, Bippus & Barrington, Inc.

Sharon Gray, decorative painter, took assignments at Jessup Inc. for all kinds of faux finishing.

Paul Maybaum, draper, made curtains for Jessup Inc. in Palm Beach.

Mimi Maddock McMakin (b. 1947) joined the interior design department of Jessup Inc. as a contractor in 1977 and stayed nine years before launching her own company. "What I learned from Mrs. Jessup was to make things gracious and comfortable, not stuffy," she said. "People have children and dogs."

Carole Douglass is an interior designer who worked with her friends Mimi McMakin and Sunny Bippus at Jessup Inc. on contractor (see "Color It Palm Beach," *House & Garden*. August 1983).

Karna Salmon (1914–unknown), an Australian-born lampshade maker, was never a Jessup Inc. employee but a contractor who used the New York office as her work room. Salmon's hand-sewn lampshades were, like Jessup Inc. curtains, first made of paper and assessed for scale. Then the linen or silk (pleated, if necessary) was applied to the frame, and a lining was added. She dyed her fantastical trims in the Jessup Inc. office kitchen. Every strand of braid on the lampshade mattered to Salmon. The unusual arrangement with Jessup Inc. kept Salmon from being poached by other designers. Mario Buatta, for example, tried to cajole Salmon into taking his commissions. To the amusement of the office staffers he would shout up the stairs, "Miss Fish, Miss Fish, may I come up?"

Notes

1. Thanks to Louis Bofferding for spotting these and the Jean Luce trays.

SELECTED BIBLIOGRAPHY

Jessup Inc.: editorial credits in which the company is named

"Toward Blue Horizons: The Florida Home of Mr. Henry Ford's Daughter at Hobe Sound" [*sic*, Josephine Kanzler was the sister of Henry Ford's daughter-in-law], *House & Garden*. September 1939. 48–49.

"Ideas to Let, and Ideas as Furnishings for the Summer House" [Tips from Billy Baldwin], *Vogue*. April 15, 1945. 63–65, 126, 128.

Gladys Freeman, "Planned for Leisure" [Theodore Weicker house], *Town & Country*. January 1955. 42–53.

Freeman, "Bamboo in Hobe Sound" [Lucien Strong house], *Town & Country*. November 1955. 76–81.

Freeman, "In the Style of Louis XVI," *Town & Country*. May 1961. 83–84.

"Scene Changers to Make Your Summer at Home as a Lark Abroad," *House & Garden*. June 1964. 92–103 with Mimi Rand of Jessup Inc., 100–101.

Curtis Besinger, "What the Bermudian House Has to Offer Us" [Swenson house in Coral Gables], *House Beautiful*. March 1964. 156–60, 172.

"Found Space for Your Three-Dimensional Treasures" [Richard McKay of Jessup, Inc.], *House & Garden*. July 1965. 102.

"Summer Living in Southampton" [William K. Laughlin house by Mimi Rand of Jessup, Inc.], *House & Garden*. August 1965. 96–111.

"Great Houses of Palm Beach" [Rodman de Heeren's Louwana and Harold Sweatt houses], *Town & Country*. February 1966. 94–97.

"Color It Palm Beach" [Paul Maddock house by Carole Douglass, Sunny Bippus, and Mimi Maddock McMakin of Jessup, Inc.], *House & Garden*. August 1983. 74–83.

Barbara Goldsmith, "Architecture: Robert A. M. Stern. Bold Forms on the Slope of Aspen's Red Mountain" [Eleanor and Frederic Bourke house], *Architectural Digest*. June 1992. 116–23, 190.

Pauline ("Polly") Daniel Jessup

Aronson, Steven M. L., "Scott Snyder, Classical Overtones for the Designer's Palm Beach House," *Architectural Digest*. September 2004. 256–63, 297.

Baldwin, Billy, with Michael Gardine, *An Autobiography*. Boston: Little, Brown and Company, 1985.

Baldwin, Billy, *Billy Baldwin Remembers*. New York: Harcourt, Brace, Jovanovich, 1974.

Douglas, Murray, and Chippy Irvine, *Brunschwig & Fils Style*. Boston, New York: Little, Brown and Company, 1995 (includes a small amount of information about Douglas's time as assistant to Jessup).

Lewis, Adam, *The Great Lady Decorators*. New York: Rizzoli 2009.

Lewis, Adam, *Billy Baldwin: The Great American Decorator*. New York: Rizzoli, 2009.

Schiro, Anne-Marie. "Grande Dame of Palm Beach Decorators," *New York Times*. March 5, 1987.

Tate, Allen, and C. Ray Smith, *Interior Design in the 20th Century*. New York: Harper & Row, 1987.

Taste

Abbott, James A., and Elaine Rice Bachman, *Designing Camelot: The Kennedy White House Restoration*. New York: Van Nostrand Reinhold, 1998.

Aldrich Jr., Nelson W., *Old Money: The Mythology of Wealth in America*. New York: Allworth Press, 1988, 1996.

Alsop, Joseph, with Adam Platt, *I've Seen The Best of It: A Memoir*. New York, London: W. W. Norton & Company, 1992.

Amory, Cleveland, *Who Killed Society?* New York: Harper & Brothers, 1960.

Baldwin, Billy, *Billy Baldwin Decorates*. New York: Holt, Rinehart and Winston, 1972.

Baltzell, E. Digby, *The Protestant Establishment*. New York: Vintage Press, 1964, 1966.

Bayley, Stephen, *Taste: The Secret Meaning of Things*. London: Faber & Faber, Circa Press, 1991, 2017.

Bender, Marylin, with Monsieur Marc, *Nouveau is Better Than No Riche at All*. New York: G. P. Putnam's Sons, 1983.

Beran, Michel Knox, *WASPS: The Splendors and Miseries of an American*

Aristocracy. New York: Pegasus Books, 2021.

Chase, Edna Woolman, and Ilka Chase, *Always in Vogue*. Garden City, NY: Country Life Press, 1954.

Crisp, Quentin, "Taste Be Damned," *House & Garden*. Vol. 161, Nos. 7–12. August 1989. 90–91.

Dunne, Dominick, *People Like Us*. New York: Crown Publishers, 1988.

Erlich, Henry, and James Hansen, "The Many Faces of Palm Beach," *Look*. February 13, 1962. 26–48.

Freund, Thatcher, *Objects of Desire: The Lives of Antiques and Those Who Pursue Them*. New York: Pantheon Books, 1993.

Harris, Diana, *Little White Houses: How the Postwar Home Constructed Race in America*. Minneapolis, London: University of Minnesota Press, 2013.

Jasanoff, Maya, "Ancestor Worship: Where Does the Craze for Genealogy Come From?" *The New Yorker*. May 9, 2022. 69–73.

Jayne, Thomas, *The Finest Rooms in America*. New York: The Monacelli Press, 2010.

McNeil, Peter, and Giorgio Riello, *Luxury: A Rich History*. Oxford: Oxford University Press, 2016.

"Palm Beach Servants Tell All," *Town & Country*. May 1972.

Pollack, Eileen S., "Furnishing Community: The Role of Margolis Furniture in the Lives of Hartford's Gentile and Jewish Families, 1920–1970." MA thesis, Cooper Hewitt National Design Museum and Parsons School of Design, 2004.

Post, Emily, *Etiquette*. New York: Funk & Wagnalls Company, 1937.

Tiffany & Co. [Letitia Baldrige], *Tiffany Table Settings*. New York: Bramhall House, The Viking Press, 1960.

Tweed, Katharine, *The Finest Rooms by America's Great Decorators*. New York: Bramhall House, The Viking Press, 1964.

Varney, Carleton, *The Draper Touch*. New York: Prentice Hall Press, 1988.

Wolfe, Elsie de [Ruby Ross Wood], *The House in Good Taste*. New York: Rizzoli, 1913, 2004.

Wharton, Edith, *A Backward Glance*. New York: Touchstone, Simon & Schuster, 1933, 1998.

Wharton, Edith, and Ogden Codman Jr., *The Decoration of Houses*. New York: Classical American Edition, The Arthur Ross Foundation, W. W. Norton, 1897, 1978, 1997.

Wilkerson, Isabel, *Caste: The Origins of Our Discontents*. New York: Random House, 2020.

Clients

Amory, Cleveland, *The Last Resorts*. New York: Harper & Row, 1948, 1952.

Ash, Jennifer, *Private Palm Beach: Tropical Style*. New York: Abbeville Press, 1992.

Bricker, Lauren Weiss, *The Mediterranean House in America*. New York: Abrams, 2008.

Bridenstine, James A., *Edsel & Eleanor Ford House*. Grosse Pointe Shores, MI: Edsel & Eleanor Ford House, 1988.

Curl, Donald W., "The Florida Architecture of F. Burrall Hoffman Jr., 1882–1980," *The Florida Historical Quarterly*, Vol. 76, No. 4, 1997. 399–416.

Curl, Donald, "Introduction." In *Florida Architecture of Addison Mizner*. New York: William Helburn, 1928, New York: Dover Publications, 1992. 1–22.

Curl, Donald, *A. Mizner's Florida: American Resort Architecture*. The Architectural Foundation, New York. Cambridge, MA: The MIT Press, 1984.

Curtis, Charlotte, *The Rich and Other Atrocities*. New York: Harper & Row, 1976.

Day, Jane, *From Palm Beach to Shangri La: The Architecture of Marion Sims Wyeth*. Preservation Foundation of Palm Beach. New York: Rizzoli, 2021.

Duchin, Peter, with Charles Michener, *Ghost of a Chance*. New York: Random House, 1996.

The Estate of Ambassador Pamela Harriman. New York: Sotheby's, May 19–21, 1997.

Goldsmith, Barbara, "Architecture: Robert A. M. Stern. Bold Forms on the Slope of Aspen's Red Mountain," *Architectural Digest*. June 1992. 116–23, 190.

Griswold, Mac, *I'll Build a Stairway to Paradise: A Life of Bunny Mellon*. New York: Farrar, Straus and Giroux, 2022.

Hoffstot, Barbara, *Landmark Architecture of Palm Beach*. Pittsburgh: Ober Park Associates, 1974.

Jolly, Anna, "Eine Villa für die Kunst: der Wohnsitz von Margaret und Werner Abegg in Riggisberg," *Kunst + Architektur der Schweiz*. Vol. 70, No. 1, 2020. 12–20.

Kazanjian, Dodie, "Inside Newport," *House & Garden*. August 1989. 54–67, 143.

Keyes, Emelie, "Two Hundred Years in Ten Minutes is the Record Being Made by Jessup," *The Palm Beach Post*, September 13, 1931.

Lambert, Gerard Barnes, *All Out of Step*. New York: Doubleday, 1956.

Mellon, Peter, with John Baskett, *Reflections in a Silver Spoon: A Memoir*. New York: William Morrow and Company, 1992.

Mockler, Kim I., *Maurice Fatio: Palm Beach Architect*. New York: Acanthus Press, 2010.

Nelson, James Carl, *Five Lieutenants: The Heartbreaking Story of Five Harvard Men Who Led America to Victory in World War I* [McKinlock]. New York: St. Martin's Griffin, 2012.

Pitcher, George, *A Life of Grace: The Biography of Grace Lansing Lambert*. Princeton, NJ: Grace Lansing Lambert, 1987.

Property from the Collection of Josephine and Walter Buhl Ford II. New York: Sotheby's, October 6, 2006.

Property from the Collection of Mrs. Charles Wrightsman Removed From Her Palm Beach Residence. New York: Sotheby's, May 5, 1984.

Roberts, Ellen E., with contributions by Lesley A. Wolff, *Ralph Norton and His Museum*. West Palm Beach: Norton Museum of Art, 2019.

Smith, Liz, *Dishing: Great Dish and Dishes from America's Most Beloved Gossip Columnist*. New York: Simon & Schuster, 2005.

Stanfill, Sonnet, *The Glamour of Italian Fashion Since 1945*. London: Victoria and Albert Museum, 2014.

Travers, J. Wadsworth, *Beautiful Palm Beach*. 1929.

Volk, Lillian Jane, Lory Armstrong Volk, and William Dale Waters, *John L. Volk: Palm Beach Architect*. Palm Beach: John L. Volk Foundation, 2001.

Weeks, Christopher, *The Life and Gardens of Harvey Ladew*. Baltimore: Johns Hopkins University Press, 1999.

CLIENT LIST

Margaret and Werner Abegg, New York; Adsit; Albee [probably Frances, Mrs. Reed, Palm Beach]; Mrs. Maitland Alexander, Palm Beach; Calvin Allen; Mrs. Melvin Alpern, Palm Beach; Asplundh; Mrs. Frederic Ayers, Gulf Stream; Baker, Palm Beach; Mr. and Mrs. Pierre Bailly, Gulf Stream; Billy Baldwin, New York; Mrs. Amalie Baruch Banks, Boca Raton; Baraban [probably Peter, Palm Beach]; Martha and W. Stanton Barbour, Palm Beach; Bath & Tennis Club, Palm Beach; Mrs. Robert Belknap, Hobe Sound; Howard Bell, Palm Beach; George Berlinger, Hollywood, Florida; Anthony "Tony" Drexel Biddle Jr., Palm Beach; Mrs. Bienecke; Harry P. Bingham, Palm Beach; Shirley and Conrad Black, Palm Beach, Toronto; J. A. Boult; Mrs. Yelverton Bolles, Palm Beach; Mrs. Bontecue, Palm Beach, Millbrook; Mrs. Gerard Bos; Mrs. Frederic Bourke Jr., Aspen; C. Brokow, Long Island; Mrs. Archibald Brown of McMillan, Inc., New York; Mr. and Mrs. Leavitt Bulkley; Burroughs; Butts; Candler, Grosse Pointe; Walter S. Carpenter, Hobe Sound; Chamberlain; Mrs. Randolph Churchill; Mrs. Saul Z. Cohen, Larchmont; Mrs. Jeffrey Cole; Mrs. George Coleman, Palm Beach; Isabel and Miles Collier, Hobe Sound; Henry Course, Hobe Sound; Jean Morton and Joseph Cudahy, Palm Beach; Cummings; Danford; Mrs. Nellie Payne Darling; Jack Davidson, Palm Beach; Mrs. Bedford Davie, Palm Beach, Scottsdale, AZ; Detroit Institute of Arts, Michigan; Phyllis and C. Douglas Dillon, Hobe Sound; Hugo Dixon, Hobe Sound; Wesley Dixon Jr.; Jessie Woolworth and James P. Donahue, Palm Beach; Douglass, Palm Beach; Albert B. Drake, Palm Beach; Oliver B. Drake; Mrs. Henry DuBois, Hobe Sound; Joseph Dumphy; Margery Durant, Palm Beach; du Pont, Palm Beach; H. T. Dyett, Hobe Sound; James Edwards, Lost Tree; Van Horn Ely, Hobe Sound; Everglades Club, Palm Beach; Mrs. Thomas Ewing, Palm Beach; Mrs. Edgar Eyre, Palm Beach; Emelia Fanjul, Palm Beach; Mrs. Marshall Field Jr.; Edith and Benson Ford, Grosse Pointe, Palm Beach, *Onika* yacht, New York; Eleanor and Edsel Ford, *Onika* yacht, Grosse Pointe, Seal Harbor; Anne and Henry Ford II, Grosse Pointe, Palm Beach, Southampton; Marylou and John B. Ford, Hobe Sound; Josephine and Walter Buhl Ford, Grosse Pointe, Seal Harbor; Martha and William Clay Ford, Grosse Pointe, Easthampton; Fortune; Foshay; Mrs. E. Fouts, Houston; Fowler; Mrs. Andrew Fraser, Palm Beach; Frost; Mrs. Cyrus Fulton, Gammage; Bernice Chrysler and Edgar W. Garbisch, Palm Beach; Mrs. Edward Garrett, Palm Beach; Mrs. George Garrett, Washington, DC, Palm Beach; Bradley Gaylord; Gerry; Clarence Geist, Palm Beach; Mrs. Gettney; Getty, Palm Beach; Eles (Liz) Gillet, Palm Beach; Mrs. Philip Glatfelter, Philadelphia; Jacqueline and Nathan Goldman, Palm Beach; Gottesman; Mrs. Ormond Gould; Mr. and Mrs. J. Peter Grace; Helen Gray, Lost Tree; Mrs. Bowman Gray, Palm Beach; Mrs. Greene; Mrs. Paul E. Greer, Hobe Sound; Oscar Gren, Lake Worth, Palm Beach; Mrs. Winston Guest, Palm Beach; Gloria and Loel Guinness, Manalapan; Mrs. Theo Griggs, Palm Beach; Gunster, Palm Beach; Mrs. Frederick Gwinner; Mrs. Averell Harriman, Hobe Sound, Middleburg, VA; Mrs. Hal Hall, Chattanooga, Lookout Mountain, TN; Mr. and Mrs. Fred Hamilton, Hobe Sound; William Hamm, Hobe Sound; Hanley, Palm Beach; Hardeen; Mrs. W. C. Harris, Palm Beach; Mrs. Robert Hartman, Chicago; Judge and Mrs. A. G. Hartridge, Palm Beach; George Headley, Palm Beach; Aimée and Rodman de Heeren, Palm Beach; Hemmes; Hoffman; Holbrook, Palm Beach; Alben Holder; Mrs. Richard Holson, Elk Hill, VA; Nelson H. Howe, Boca Raton; Helen Huntington Hull; Russell Hull, Palm Beach; Huntington; Mrs. Harry Hurst, Delray Beach; Marjorie and E. F. Hutton, Palm Beach; Idle Hour Country Club, Lexington, KY; Mrs. John Ingle; Mrs. Hubert James, Hobe Sound; Jennings; Jergens, Palm Beach; Mrs. Allen Johnson, Birmingham, AL; Mrs. Crawford Johnson, Hobe Sound; Virginia Johnson, Palm Beach; Walter J. Johnson, Philadelphia; Mrs. Frederick E. Jones, Hobe Sound, Fishers Island; Jupiter Island Inn and Club; Josephine and Ernest Kanzler, Hobe Sound, Grosse Pointe, Seal Harbor; Mrs. Robert Kanzler; Mrs. Don Kelley, Palm Beach; Kennedy, Palm Beach; Edith and Hugh Kirkland, Palm Beach; Mrs. William Koch, Delray Beach; Stanleigh Krewson, Philadelphia; Harvey Ladew, Gulf Stream; Grace and Gerard Lambert, Manalapan; Alexandra and Alfonso Landa, Palm Beach; Mrs. Morton Lane, Palm Beach; Lansing, Nassau; Mrs. William Laporte; William K. Laughlin, Southampton; Estée and Joseph Lauder, Palm Beach; Dr. and Mrs. Lennan; Irma and Louis Sampter Levy, Palm Beach; Blanche Paley and Dr. Leon Levy, Palm Beach; Rawson G. Lizars, Palm Beach; Mrs. John Lord, Hobe Sound; Mrs. Randolph Lothrop, Palm Beach; Mrs. Tyson Lykes, Palm Beach; Stephen Lyras; Susan P. and William J. McAneeny, Palm Beach; Mrs. McCarty, Delray Beach; Albert McConnell, Hobe Sound; Mrs. Gladys McCormick-Goodhart, Hobe Sound; McGinnis, Palm Beach; Merrill McGowan, Palm

Beach; Marion McKinlock, Palm Beach; Mrs. James McGraw, Hobe Sound; Mrs. James McGraw II, Palm Beach; McNeil, Hobe Sound; Maddock, Palm Beach; Marguano, Hobe Sound; Marshmann, Palm Beach; Chan and John Mashek, Newport, RI; John Mascherini, New York; Harold Masten, Palm Beach; Matheson; Mr. and Mrs. A. H. Meadows, Palm Beach; Mrs. Edward Meister, Hobe Sound; Melhado, New York; Mary and Paul Mellon, Hobe Sound; Jane and Matthew Mellon, Jamaica; Mrs. George Merck, Hobe Sound; Mrs. Houghton P. Metcalf, Hobe Sound; David Meyer, Palm Beach; Mrs. Jeremiah Millbank; Mrs. Harry C. Mills, New York; Mrs. Herbert Morris, Cape Cod; Mrs. Alfred Morse; Leonard Mudge, Manalapan; Virginia and Ector Munn, Palm Beach; Robert P. Noble, Hobe Sound; Norris, Hobe Sound; Elizabeth and Ralph Norton, Palm Beach; Mrs. Nicholas Noyes, Hobe Sound; Lady Eunice and Sir Harry Oakes, Palm Beach, Bar Harbor, Nassau; Oelsner; Mrs. Spencer Olin, New York, Hobe Sound, St. Louis; Mr. and Mrs. Charles Oliver, Chapel Hill, NC; Ordway; Parker; Mary Parlett; Bryson Payne; Joan Whitney Payson, Hobe Sound; Peterson, Hobe Sound; Pettit; Mrs. Phipps, Palm Beach; Eleanor and John S. Pillsbury, Palm Beach; Boone Porter, Palm Beach; Violet and Clarence Prentice, Delray Beach; Prescott, Greenwich, Hobe Sound; Gladys Pulitzer Preston, New York, Washington, DC; Mrs. Price; Mrs. John Prosser; Pulitzer, Palm Beach; Raiss; Raley, Palm Beach; Lady Ramsey, Hobe Sound; Byron Ramsing, Palm Beach; Thor Ramsing, Palm Beach; Mr. and Mrs. James Rand, Stuart; Mrs. George Rasmussen; William A. Read Jr. and Isabel Collier Read, Palm Beach; Permelia and Joseph V. Reed, Hobe Sound, Greenwich; Nathaniel Reed, Hobe Sound; Verner Z. Reed, Hobe Sound; Mrs. Joseph Regenstein, Palm Beach, Chicago, Miami; Reighly, Hobe Sound, Connecticut; Rentschler, Boca Raton; Reymer; W. R. Reynolds, Palm Beach; W. R. Reynolds Jr., Palm Beach; Richards; Halstead Ritter, Palm Beach; Rooke, Palm Beach; Mrs. George Rosengarten, Hobe Sound; Mr. and Mrs. Ruckelhaus, Indianapolis; Mary and Stephen ("Laddie") Sanford, Palm Beach; Dr. William Sayed, Palm Beach, Chicago; Scheerer, Hobe Sound; Horace Schmidlapp, Palm Beach; Mrs. John Searle, Hobe Sound, Chicago, Winnetka, Lake Forest; Edmond Sheedy; Frederick Sears, Palm Beach; Jesse Shaughnessy, Palm Beach; Irene and Alfred P. Sloan, Palm Beach; Marion Margery and Worthington Scranton, Hobe Sound; Mrs. Allen Shelden, Grosse Pointe; Mrs. Allen Shelden Jr.; Mrs. Thomas Shevlin, Palm Beach; Mrs. Earl E. T. Smith, Palm Beach; Mrs. Maynard Smith, Palm Beach; Snowden; Mrs. Spielman; Mrs. Spencer, Palm Beach; Daniel Stack, Palm Beach, Grosse Pointe; V. B. Steinbough, Palm Beach; Mrs. R. P. Stevens, Hobe Sound; Mrs. Robert Stott, Palm Beach, New York; Mrs. Stowell; Lucien Strong, Hobe Sound; Sudbrink; Mrs. Harold Sweatt; Jessie and Edward F. Swenson Sr., Palm Beach; Mrs. Edward F. Swenson Jr., Miami; Robert Hudson Tannahill, Grosse Pointe; Tat Saunders, Palm Beach; Mrs. Morgan Taylor, Hobe Sound; O. N. Tevander, Palm Beach; Harry Thomas, Palm Beach; D. Thompson; Mrs. William Tiernan; Mrs. Edward Townsend; Mrs. Trout, Palm Beach; Carll Tucker, Hobe Sound; Mrs. Howell Van Gerbig, Palm Beach; Van Husan, Palm Beach; Vietor, Palm Beach; Mr. and Mrs. Kenneth Van Ripper, Palm Beach; Mrs. L. Wadmond; Mr. and Mrs. Samuel Walker, Stuart; Helen Wilshire Walsh, Hobe Sound; Rodman Wanamaker, Palm Beach; Barclay Warburton, Palm Beach; Janet and William Watt; Reginald Webster; Mrs. Theodore Weicker, Hobe Sound, New York; Mrs. Oliver Wellington, Pompano; Joseph Werner, Palm Beach; Mrs. Frederick Weyerhauser, Hobe Sound; Mrs. Robert White; Betsy and Jock Whitney, New York, Long Island, Georgia; Diana Strawbridge Wister, Palm Beach; Ruby Ross Wood; Woodward, Palm Beach; Mrs. Charles Wrightsman, Palm Beach.

ABOUT THE AUTHOR

Cultural historian Maggie Lidz writes and researches on a broad spectrum of twentieth-century social history. For ten years, she was the historian at the Winterthur Museum, Garden and Library. Although best known as a museum of American decorative arts, Winterthur's horticultural, architectural, and social history was fertile territory for investigation. . From March 2016 to March 2017, she worked as a research consultant to the Edsel & Eleanor Ford House in Grosse Pointe, Michigan, where she first learned of Jessup Inc. On December 17, 2017 she published an article, "The Decorator Time Almost Forgot," in *Architectural Digest* about the exhibition at the Preservation Foundation of Palm Beach on Polly Jessup. She and her husband now live in Ojai, California.

Lidz graduated from Columbia with a BA in history and from the University of Delaware with an MA in art history. Her master's thesis was on the architectural development of Winterthur, the du Pont family's house. She has published numerous articles in magazines including *The Magazine Antiques*, *Antiques and Fine Art*, and *Southern Living*. Her books include *Life at Winterthur: A du Pont Family Album* (2001), *The du Ponts: Houses and Gardens on the Brandywine* (Acanthus Press, 2009), and *The du Ponts of Winterthur* (2013). She co-curated the 2015 Winterthur exhibit *Tiffany: The Color of Luxury* and the most successful exhibition in Winterthur's sixty-year history, *The Costumes of Downton Abbey* (March 2013-January 2014).

INDEX

Page numbers in *italics* refer to illustrations

Abegg, Werner and Peggy 58, 59
Adams, Carl 68
Adams, Henry 11
Akintievsky, Zina *40*
Alavoine 48
Astor, Vincent 59

Baldwin, Billy 9–10, 39, 53, *54*, 67, 70
Bassett, Marie 62
Bath & Tennis Club, Palm Beach 36, *47*
Beaton, Cecil 39
Becker, Martin 48
Belknap, Maitland 67
Berenson, Bernard 11
Bermudes, Skip 10, 68
Biddle, Anthony Joseph Drexel Jr. ("Tony") 17, 20
Bigelow, Ruth Campbell 25
Bippus, Margaret Caroline ("Sunny") 72
Black, Conrad and Shirley 41, 69
Blair, Wolcott 37
Bourke, Frederic 10
Braden, Jack 68
Bradley's Beach Club, Palm Beach 36
Bretz, Carl August *40*, 68
Bridenstine, James 64, 66
Brooks, Hank 68
Brown, Eleanor McMillen 39
Brunschwig & Fils *48*, *66*
Buatta, Mario 72
Burden, Carter 70

Caler, Kemp 39, 67
Canaday, John 57
Carlhian of Paris 10, 48
Casa della Porta, Palm Beach 25, *26*
Cézanne, Paul 57, *58*
Chaplin, Charlie 19
Christie, Sir Harold G. 59, 68
Churchill, Pamela 39
Cochran, Henry 68–9
Codman, Ogden Jr. 29, 31
Colby, Anita 70
Colefax and Fowler 9
Coon, John ("Jack") 69
Copeland, Pamela Cunningham 41
Corse, Henry 45, 46, 50–1
Coward, Noel 55

Dame, Ray B. *22*
Daniel, David 11, 13, 14
Daniel, David Richard 11, 13
Daniel, Harry 14
Daniels, Margaret Harrington 13, 15, 17, 59
Dave Daniel's Modern Clothes Shop 14–15, *14*, 25
de Wolfe, Elsie 29, 31, 67, 68
Detroit Institute of Arts *40*, 56, 57
Dillon, C. Douglas and Phyllis 62, *62*
Disney, Walt 39
Donahue, Jessie 24
Doughty, Dorothy *64*
Douglass, Carole 72
Draper, Dorothy 44
du Pont, Henry Francis 31, 33
Dunne, Dominick 36, 41
Dunstan, George and Mildred 20
Duveen, Lord 44

Edsel and Eleanor Ford House 10, 64–6, *64*, *65*, *66*
Eisenhower, Dwight D. 62, *62*
Elizabeth, Queen Mother 31
Euler, E. Reeves 20
Everglades Club, Palm Beach 36, 38, 43

Fairbanks, Douglas 19
Farley, Elsie Sloan 24
Fatio, Maurice 17, 20, 25, 38, 67
Faulkner, Edward D. 25
Fereira, Dulce 69
First National Bank *21*, 50
Fitzgerald, F. Scott 13
Foote, Louise 16, 17, 18, 20
Ford, Edsel 36, 45, 48–50, *49*, 60, 64–6, *64*, *65*, *66*
Ford, Eleanor 10, 45, 48–50, *49*, 56, 60, 64–6, *64*, *65*, *66*
Ford, Eleanor "Nonie" 10
Ford, Henry and Anne 31, 60, *60*, *61*, *63*
Ford, John B., and Marylou *30*
Ford, Josephine 31
Fowler, John 39
French & Company 10

Galloway, Katharine 11, 13
Garbisch, Bernice Chrysler 31, 69
Garbisch, Edgar 69, 70
Geist, Clarence 25
Ginsburg & Levy 39
Gish, Lillian 44
Goldberg, Rube 24
Graham, Katharine 62
Gray, Sharon 72
Griffith, D. W. 19
Guest, Frederick and Amy 36
Guinness, Loel and Gloria 55

H & D Daniel Clothing 14
Halbert, Edith 56
Hamm, William Jr. 47, *47*, 48
Hammell, John 66
Harriman, Averell 13
Harriman, Pamela 39, 41
Heintz, Joseph the Younger *58*
Historical Society of Palm Beach County 10, 18, 43
Hoffman, F. Burrall Jr. 59, 67
Holland, Flanders 69
Horsfall, Morland 17, 20
Horsfall, Ruth 17
Howell, Josephine 39
Hudson, Joseph L. 56
Hulse, John 10, 68, 69, 72

Jessup, Elon 36
Jessup, John Colgate Jr. 16–18, *17*, 19–20, 36, *36*
  death 38, 64
  Jessup Inc. 20, 24, 25, 34, 35, 46
Jessup Inc. 10, *12*, 20–35
  6100 Georgia Avenue 33, 44, 51
  carvings 22, 28
  door designs 22, 23
  employees 67–72
  furniture 24, 27, 33, 38–9, 51, 51, 59
  New York arm 39
  postwar years 38–9
  World War II 37
Johnson, Virginia Campbell 55, *55*, 59, *59*, 67–8
Johnson, William Royster 55, 59, *59*, 67, 68
Johnson and Faulkner (Jofa) 25
Jupiter Island Club, Hobe Sound 36–7, 46, 67

Kanzler, Ernest and Josephine 44–5, *46*, 56
Kay, Alfred and Elizabeth 44
Kennedy, Jacqueline 31, 33, 39
Kirkland, Hugh and Edith 53, *54*, 67
Koehler, Henry *71*
Kort, Susanna ("Sadie") 68
Kuhn, Walt 46–7

la Fresnaye, Robert de *57*
La Mésangère, Pierre de *34*
LaCagnina, Henry *47*
Ladew, Harvey 41
Lambert, Gerard ("Jerry") and Grace 53–5, *55*
Landa, Alfonso and Alexandra 64
Lanfranchi, Anne 38, 46
Lange, Medard 66
Langlois, Pierre-Eloi *63*
Lauder, Estée 50, 62, 69
Lawrence, William 25
Levy, Louis and Irma 44, *45*
Lewis, Adam 10
Lewis, Sinclair 31, 33
Lord & Taylor 69
Louis, Prince of Battenberg 28
Luce, Jean 44

McAneeny, William J. 25, *50*
McCormick-Goodhart, Frederick 48
McCormick-Goodhart, Gladys 48, *48*
McGinnis, Neal 10, 41, 43, 69, 70
McKay, Richard 69–70
McKim, Mead & White 28
McMakin, Mimi Maddock 11, 38, 41, 70, 72
McMillen Inc. 10, 60
Marin, John 56
Martin, Hilda Stewart 69
Mascheroni, John 39
Mashek, John and Chan 69
Maugham, Syrie 44, *45*
Maybaum, Paul 72
Mayhew, Billy 69
Meacham, Malcolm 17, 20
Mellon, Bunny 33
Mellon, Mary Conover (Minna) 46
Mellon, Matthew and Jane Bartram 59–60, *59*
Mizner, Addison 21, 22, *22*, 24, 25, 36, 44, 67
Mizner Industries 21–2
Mussolini, Benito 59

Nast, Condé 29
National Trust 39
Norton, Ralph and Elizabeth 51
Norton Gallery and School of Art 51, *51*, 67, 69

Oakes, Sir Harry 59, 68
O'Keefe, Georgia 56
Olympia Improvement Corporation 17, 18–19
Olympia-Picture City 19, 45

Pahlmann, William 69
Palm Beach National Bank 20
Parish, Sister 15, 31, 36, 39, 70
Parzinger, Tommi 39
Paseo Palmera, West Palm Beach *36*
Payson, Charles and Joan 70
Peck, Gregory 13
Peck, Susan 25
Pepper, Anne 39, 70
Peters, Edward C. 21–2
Phipps Plaza, Palm Beach *8*, *40*, 62, *63*
Picasso, Pablo *56*, 57
Pickford, Mary 19
Post, Emily 28, 29, 31
Post, Marjorie Merriweather 43
Prentice, Clarence and Violet 59, *59*
Preservation Foundation of Palm Beach 10, 39
Preston, Gladys Pulitzer 70

Rain, Charles 69
Rand, Mimi 69, 70, *71*
Rathbone, Perry Townsend 56
Reagan, Nancy 41
Reagan, Ronald 41
Reed, Joseph Verner *28*, 36–7, 38, 45–7, 48
Reed, Permelia 17, *28*, 36–7, 38, 45–7, 48, 50–1, 66
Reif, Rita 69–70
Robertson, William P. ("Robby") 70
Rockefeller, Abby Aldrich 56
Roosevelt, Eleanor 15
Rothstein, Arnold 13
Rouault, Georges 57, *57*

Salmon, Karna 72
Sanger, Margaret 15–16, 18
Saunders, Catherine ("Tat") 53, *53*
Saunders, Mary 53
Scalamandré *57*
Schenck, Joseph 18–19
Schiro, Anne-Marie 10
Scranton, Worthington and Marion Margery 51, *52*
Sears, Frederick and Norma 67
Selznick, Lewis J. 18–19
Shaughnessy, Francis A. 50
Sheeler, Charles 56
Simonson, Byron 39
Sloan, Alfred P. and Irene 37
Smith, Wallace Herndon *63*
Smith & Watson 39
Stern, Robert A. M. 10
Swenson, Edward F. *4*, 50, 62, *62*
Swenson, Jessie Shaughnessy *4*, 50, *50*, *51*, 62, *62*

Tannahill, Robert Hudson 45, 56–7, *57*
Tat Saunders 53, *53*
Teague, Walter 48–9
Termina, Nina 70
Thomas, Edgar R. ("Eddie") 69, 70
Trump, Donald 43
Trump, Ivana 43
Tucker, Carll 50–1, *51*

Valentiner, William R. 56
Van Gol, Hattie 39
Van Riper, Kenneth and Beatrice 25
Vanderbilt, Harold ("Mike") 44
Vanderbilt family 29, 31, 43
Vanderwaeren, Marie ("Mip") J. 70
Volk, John 39, 59, 62, *64*
Volunteers for Victory 37–8, *37*

Wanamaker, Rodman 25
Warburton, Barclay 25
Weber, Joseph F. 51, 68, 70
West, Mabel 35
Wharton, Edith 13, 29, 31
The White House, Washington 28, 31, 33, 39, 41
Whitney, Betsy and John Hay 70
Whitney, Marie 13
Wideman, Lois 43, 72
Wilcox, Ray 68, 70
Williams, Harrison and Mona 44, *45*
Windsor, Duchess of 31
Wister, Diana Strawbridge 41
Wolfe, Tom 24
Wood, Ruby Ross 10, 31, 67
Worrell, Ben 48
Wrightsman, Jayne 31, 39
Wyeth, King & Johnson 59, *59*
Wyeth, Marion Sims 24, 39, *53*, 54–5, 59, 67

Ziegfeld, Florenz 44